# The Secrets of Planning and Designing a Hand-Hooked Rug: Your Complete Guide to Planning & Designing Rugs

by Deanne Fitzpatrick with Susan Huxley

**Standing Before the Monument,** 8' x 6'; #6-, #8-cut wool, hand-cut wool, and hand-spun yarns on Scottish burlap. Designed and hooked by Deanne Fitzpatrick, Amherst, Nova Scotia, Canada; 2002. From the collection of Arif Samad.

DEDICATION

*To Adele and Mikhial, who help me look at things with fresh
eyes every day because they are young enough to know that creativity
is part of being, and that art is all around us.*

# Table of Contents

*From the Editor* . . . . . . . . . . . . . . . . . . . . . . . . . . . . . . . . . . . . . . . . . .3

*About the Author* . . . . . . . . . . . . . . . . . . . . . . . . . . . . . . . . . . . . . . . . 3

*Introduction: Walk in a Glorious Garden . . . Dream of Magnificence* . . . . . . . . . . . 4

*Chapter One: Great Beginnings* . . . . . . . . . . . . . . . . . . . . . . . . .5
   • Collecting Supplies and Tools . . . . . . . . . . . . . . . . . . . . . .6
   • Overcoming Fears . . . . . . . . . . . . . . . . . . . . . . . . . . . . . .9
   • Developing Basic Drawing Skills . . . . . . . . . . . . . . . . . . . .12

*Chapter Two: Original Design Plan* . . . . . . . . . . . . . . . . . . . . . . . . . . .16
   • Finding Inspiration . . . . . . . . . . . . . . . . . . . . . . . . . . . . .17
   • Developing Content . . . . . . . . . . . . . . . . . . . . . . . . . . . .19
   • Telling Tales . . . . . . . . . . . . . . . . . . . . . . . . . . . . . . . . .21

*Chapter Three: Designing with Templates* . . . . . . . . . . . . . . . . . . .25
   • Preparing Templates . . . . . . . . . . . . . . . . . . . . . . . . . . . .26
   • Enhancing Templates . . . . . . . . . . . . . . . . . . . . . . . . . . .28
   • Creating Your Own Templates . . . . . . . . . . . . . . . . . . . . . .30

*Chapter Four: Practical Methods for Designing* . . . . . . . . . . . . . . . . . . . . . . .32
   • Planning for Location . . . . . . . . . . . . . . . . . . . . . . . . . . .33
   • Creating Great Compositions . . . . . . . . . . . . . . . . . . . . . .35
   • Conquering Perspective . . . . . . . . . . . . . . . . . . . . . . . . .37
   • Understanding Balance . . . . . . . . . . . . . . . . . . . . . . . . . .38
   • Cropping for Style . . . . . . . . . . . . . . . . . . . . . . . . . . . . .39
   • Creating a Focal Point . . . . . . . . . . . . . . . . . . . . . . . . . .40
   • Designing Dynamic Borders . . . . . . . . . . . . . . . . . . . . . . .41
   • Shaping a Rug . . . . . . . . . . . . . . . . . . . . . . . . . . . . . . . .45

*Chapter Five: Secrets of Style* . . . . . . . . . . . . . . . . . . . . . . . . . . .48
   • Understanding Style . . . . . . . . . . . . . . . . . . . . . . . . . . . .49
   • Working with Texture . . . . . . . . . . . . . . . . . . . . . . . . . . .51
   • Using Color Freely . . . . . . . . . . . . . . . . . . . . . . . . . . . . .55
   • Creating Movement . . . . . . . . . . . . . . . . . . . . . . . . . . . .59

*Chapter Six: The Gallery* . . . . . . . . . . . . . . . . . . . . . . . . . . . . . . .62

*Sources* . . . . . . . . . . . . . . . . . . . . . . . . . . . . . . . . . . . . . . . . . . .72

*About the Publisher/What is Rug Hooking?* . . . . . . . . . . . . . . . . . . . . . . .73

## The Secrets of Planning & Designing Hand-Hooked Rugs

*by Deanne Fitzpatrick with Susan Huxley*

**Editor**
*Virginia P. Stimmel*

**Book Designer**
*CW Design Solutions, Inc.*

**Assistant Editor**
*Lisa McMullen*

**Chairman**
*M. David Detweiler*

**Publisher**
*J. Richard Noel*

**Content produced by**
*Huxley Communication LLC, Easton, Pennsylvania*

**Developmental and Substantive Editor**
*Susan Huxley*

**Editoral Assistant**
*Katherine Riess*

**Photographer**
*Robert Gerheart*

*Presented by*

# H·O·O·KinG
### R·U·G

1300 Market St., Suite 202
Lemoyne, PA 17043-1420
(717) 234-5091 • (800) 233-9055
*www.rughookingonline.com*
*rughook@paonline.com*

PRINTED IN CHINA

# From the Editor

One of the most challenging aspects of starting a new project is the planning and designing process, especially if you want to create your own motif. Where do I start? Since I'm not a fine artist, how do I draw my own pattern? Where do I place the templates for a balanced look? How do I transfer the pattern onto the backing? Last year when we mailed a book survey to our readers, this topic was at the top of the list. As a result of our findings, *Rug Hooking* magazine is pleased to present our newest book, *The Secrets of Planning and Designing Hand-Hooked Rugs*—a step-by-step journey that will take you from conception to completion.

Ideas for motifs surround us in every day life—nature, home, or special moments. All we need is our imagination and favorite subjects; the rest will come. Take the guesswork out of the process. With *The Secrets of Planning and Designing Hand-Hooked Rugs* as a reference guide, the planning will no longer be intimidating. Author Deanne Fitzpatrick leads you through each of the stages and includes suggestions for how to develop motifs, different methods of transferring the pattern onto backings, how to estimate the amount of material needed, and tips and suggestions on personalizing the rug to your own tastes.

This book is an indispensable tool that you won't want to be without. Plus, the book contains full-size template patterns to get you started.

For those who doubt their artistic abilities and for those with a "can do" attitude, this beautifully illustrated book will be a guide to expanding your rug hooking horizons. Written in an easy-to-read format, each chapter of *The Secrets of Planning and Designing Hand-Hooked Rugs* will help open the door for the creative process to begin. Enjoy reading *Rug Hooking* magazine's newest addition to the rug hooking library.—*Ginny Stimmel*

## ABOUT THE AUTHOR

## Deanne Fitzpatrick

Family. Faith. Tradition. Nature. These four words are the cornerstones of Deanne Fitzpatrick's life and her art. For the dynamic, expressive works that Deanne creates in her Nova Scotia, Canada, studio are inextricably linked to every part of her world.

Hooked into the backing are the culture of her region and her personal history. Deanne's rugs express her experiences and stories to anyone who will look. It's her talent to speak with the viewer—to tell a story and express emotion—that elevates Deanne's rugs into the category of fine art.

Deanne, however, prefers to think of her work in terms of its humble beginnings, even though her pieces are found in prestigious permanent collections like The Canadian Museum of Civilization.

Deanne is a self-taught rug hooker. Although her mother and grandmother made rugs, Deanne only picked up a hook when she reached her mid-20s, in order to make "mats" for the floors of her farmhouse. After learning the basics from Marion Kennedy, Deanne realized that she had found a method of expression that met her needs. By "doing, thinking freely, reading and watching," her rug hooking evolved into personal expression.

A gentle spirit with boundless artistic talent, Deanne's rise in the rug hooking community was meteoric.

Two years after making her first rug, Deanne was represented by private galleries. The following year, she was in the juried Nova Scotia Folk Art Festival. By year four, she had her own touring solo exhibit, and rugs hooked by Deanne were in permanent public collections.

Deanne is a member of the Editorial Board of *Rug Hooking* magazine and has been the subject of a television documentary and features on national radio shows. Her credits include numerous magazines, plus two solo exhibits. Including *The Secrets of Planning and Designing Hooked Rugs*, she has authored three books.

Deanne grew up in Freshwater, Placentia Bay, Newfoundland and Labrador. She is the youngest of seven children—all girls. She now lives on the outskirts of Amherst, Nova Scotia, Canada, with her husband, son, and daughter, and elusive cat, Ash.

Her studio, By the Door Hooked Rugs, is a quaint two-story affair that's attached to the main house. If you're unable to travel to Canada's East Coast, you can enjoy her rugs and purchase patterns and other supplies through her web site www.hookingrugs.com.

# Walk in a Glorious Garden . . . Dream of Magnificence

**Getting the Rural Mail,** 48" x 64"; #6-, #8, and hand-cut wool, natural lamb's wool and silk yarn on burlap. Designed and hooked by Deanne Fitzpatrick, Amherst, Nova Scotia, Canada, 2004. From the collection of Lynn Bishop.

I wrote this book for those of you who want to create your own designs and use rug hooking as a means of self expression. The journey that you'll take is nothing to be afraid of. In fact, your creative development as a rug hooker is like a walk down the path of a glorious garden, where you get to pick a bouquet of flowers that catch your fancy.

If you want it, and if you work at it, you can design wonderful rugs that tell the story of your time in this world. I know this is true because I have watched my own rugs grow, change, and develop.

My early designs were simple. I started rug hooking as a craftsperson creating floor mats for my old farmhouse. My life as a rug hooking artist was an accidental journey. I discovered something that I liked to do more than almost anything else. I could hook for hours at a time without looking up, and I learned that I could blend existing ideas together to make new ideas that are my own.

I didn't have years of artistic experience nor a fine arts degree. I didn't even see myself as a creative person. It was only when I was in my 20s that I learned the difference between a painting that someone created by hand and the pictures that my mother had bought at a department store. I didn't grow up in a home where being an artist was even a possibility. Outside of a coloring book and crayons, there were no basic art supplies in our house. I would tear the blank sheets out of the front of my father's paperbacks when I needed drawing paper. My mother showed me how to make glue from flour and water, and there was always plenty of black electrical tape in my father's tool kit.

I suppose I could look at this childhood and think, "If only I had tools and opportunities." Or I could reflect back and say, "They taught me resourcefulness and ingenuity." I choose the latter. I tell you this because, so often, we're intimidated by artists whose journeys are well underway. We don't look at the fact that they began with their own set of circumstances and inhibitions.

Look to yourself. Accept your own ability and background. Make the very best of what you've experienced. The greatest thing you have to offer this process is your commitment of time. Whether it's your drawing skills or your wool cupboard that's limited, I encourage you take up the challenge.

Play with the ideas in this book like you had more time than sense. It's nothing more than a guide to help you develop a creative approach to design. Please use it for ideas so that you can be inspired to create, grow, and make rugs that are more magnificent than you ever dreamed they could be.

## CHAPTER ONE

# Great Beginnings

*Sometimes it can seem hard to find the inspiration for a design, and other times you may have an idea but not know how to take the next step. Yet every rug, whether it's a grand wall hanging or a basic mug mat, begins with something simple: an idea, a poem, the shape of a neighbor's house, or even a child's drawing.*

*In* The Secrets of Planning and Designing a Hand-Hooked Rug, *I'm going to guide you through the creative process.*

*The starting point is gathering supplies and tools that will make it easier for you to get started. We're not talking about anything fancy here. You'll need a hook and some wool, of course. You'll also work with sketch-books and, perhaps, a journal.*

*In this chapter, I'll also give you plenty of advice and practical ideas to ease you into the process of draw-ing. It's tempting to skip over these pages, but you might want to take a look anyway because I'm including lots of tips and suggestions that will help you have more fun.*

5

I started my hook collection during a visit to a local antique dealer. While we were chatting, I mentioned that I hook rugs. The dealer pulled out a box of 40 or 50 hooks and told me that I could have any 10, for $5 each. I was immediately drawn to the ones that had initials carved in them. The really prized ones are handmade. Hooks that were personalized by their owners are still my favorites. I love the way that the oil from a hooker's hand sinks into the wood.

Every time I visited the shop I picked up a few more hooks, then some netting needles, then a few proddy hooks . . . and so it went. Soon friends were contributing to my collection.

I don't hook with any of these treasures; they're in my studio for me to cherish. I like having them close, and they inspire me. Every time I look at the hooks and the needles I get in touch with the past. These items remind me that I'm just a small part of a long tradition of rug hooking. The art and craft of rug hooking was here long before me, and it'll still be around long after I'm gone.

My grandmother hooked mats to cover her bare floors. Hooking was something she did out of necessity, so you know that she didn't use the best hooks and frames that money could buy. But that's okay; there's more to rug hooking than the hook, scissors, and other items that make up the "craft" of hooking. What you do with your tools is more important.

The hook that I use only cost me $9. I didn't buy it because I'm cheap—it's the one that I like. To the side of my Moshimer hook, I added an adhesive-backed cushion that was designed to help people hang on to a pen. The "grab-on," as I call it, softens the blows on my fingers when I'm hooking, so I don't have any calluses.

My collection of hooks, which is shown in the photo, is humble. I'm fascinated by the ones that have character—I have one that's made from a piece of brass pipe; another started life as a knife. When it outlived its usefulness, the

owner pounded a nail in the end so that it could be used to hook rugs. I like hooks that once had another use.

As you can see, my antique hooks are all stored in a simple case. Mixed in with this collection are some proddy hooks, a dragonfly, a lobster claw, and even a piece of granite. It's important that I surround myself with inspiration and memories.

The dragonfly is there because I like it. On one of my daily walks I looked down at the ground and its shimmering wings smiled up at me. That's all the reason that I needed to bring it home. The original color of the lobster claw—a striking blue—caught my eye. Over time, the claw has faded to orange, which serves to remind me that color is really about what we see, more than color theory.

The chunk of granite is from the church that my father attended. When I was 15, I visited the abandoned village where he grew up. The marble from the alter was smashed all over the floor of the broken-down shell of the local church. I picked up the marble because it represented my roots and I brought it back to my father as a gift. Net needles, which are also in the case, are another homage to my dad, because he used to carve them from pine.

Your hands are one of your most important tools. They're an extension of who you are. You can use them to express your unique self, and *no one* can make you hook—or design—in a way that doesn't feel good to you. You'll draw the rug pattern, hold the hook, and space the loops.

The same can be said about the materials that you work with. I have my favorite backings, for example. I'm going to explain why I like them, but make up your own mind about what you prefer.

When I started rug hooking, I thought it was very important that everything stayed authentic. My backings were burlap bags that I got at a Lebanese grocery store in the Halifax, and I used recycled wool. I kept the supplies and the process as simple as possible. I didn't know my grandmother Emma Wakeham Fitzpatrick, but I've been told that she did the same thing. She would take apart a burlap bag, and then hook wool strips into it. She hooked because she wanted to . . . she couldn't resist the urge to create. When she had no old clothes to hook, she happily took apart the bags and dyed and hooked the strands of burlap onto other burlap bags.

It felt good to carry on a family tradition. Eventually, though, I was exposed to other supplies and tools. As time goes by, I learn about even more neat things. I've branched out from burlap bags—now my backing material is primitive burlap, primitive linen, and a Scottish burlap that's woven for primitive rugs.

The most important thing to look for in a backing is strength, and that the weave suits the width and weight of the strips you want to pull through. If you try to pull strips

that are too wide for the weave of the backing (a tightly woven type, for example) you'll hurt your hand and wrist. The hooking will be unpleasant.

## ▶TIP  Have Book, Will Travel

Sketch-books are in my studio, the car, and truck, beside the chair where I sit to drink my morning coffee—even beside books that I'm reading. I place a sketch-book wherever there's a chance that I'll use it. Pens and pencils go beside each sketch-book. This way, I can record an image or write down an idea whenever something strikes my fancy. If I find a pretty leaf or attractive postcard, I'll even tuck it between some pages.

## Random Thoughts On Hooking Techniques

The action of hooking a rug is really about the fingers. They have to be nimble, even though rug hooking is a visual craft. I don't think about the action a lot when I'm working at my frame.

When I hook I'm relaxed and lost in thought. I'm not thinking about every loop and how it's pulled. Instead, I'm thinking about the subject that I'm hooking or, sometimes, my mind wanders to random thoughts about life. I become immersed in what I'm doing.

I sit in a small, soft wingback chair, at a table-style frame, using a Cheticamp frame or, on occasion, a hoop. I want my burlap backing

to be very taut when I'm working on it.

As I hook, I keep my back straight. I bring the frame to me, rather than leaning over. In this way I avoid lower back troubles. I hold my hook in a loose grip. Tense muscles aren't a good thing.

I then hook the strips of wool cloth, pulling them quite high—perhaps 1/2" at times. As I hook the next loop, the one that I made gets pulled down a little bit. I try to hook in a random way. It's important to me that the rug doesn't look as if it was hooked from left to right, diagonally, or top to bottom. When finished, I want the viewer

to see the overall picture, rather than the motion of a particular area of fiber.

Granted, a roof may look like it's worked on a diagonal, or a field my have a semi-circular, sweeping motion. But the direction of the hooking will often change midstream. I do try to hook in a direction that makes sense, however. Thus, for a face, I'll fill in the cheeks, do a little of the lips, and a portion of the forehead, and then work the rest of the face. The cheeks are hooked in a circular motion, while the lips and eyes will be more linear, with a slight curve for expression.

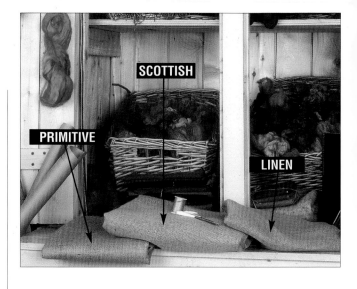

► **TIP** Plain and Simple

Whether I'm sewing a backing to my Cheticamp frame or attaching binding to a finished piece, I just use a plain, large needle.

Open weave Scottish burlap is a wonderful 70" wide fabric. It's great for doing larger pieces and I also love it for geometric patterns, because it has an even grid that makes it easier to work in straight and diagonal lines. This backing is good for finer cuts and lighter weights of cloth.

Linen is a premium backing with a relatively even grid. It works almost exactly the same way as burlap, and I like feeling its silky quality when I'm hooking into it. It's important to work on a backing that you enjoy. There's a lot of talk about the longevity of linen, yet the oldest rug in existence in Canada was hooked on burlap, surviving more than 150 years.

For practical reasons, I use primitive burlap a lot. It has an uneven grid that often works to my advantage and has a loose weave, which is excellent for hauling up thick cloths and wide cuts. I like to portray movement in my work and an uneven grid makes this easier to show.

Primitive burlap is relatively inexpensive, which makes the craft much more accessible. When teaching, I encourage my students to use it for their initial projects. However, I do encourage them to try all kinds of backings so that they find the type that they really like to work with.

There are other tools and supplies that make it easier for you to plan and design a rug: Bristolboard, permanent markers, a pen, pencils, scissors, sketch-books, wool and yarn, a T-square,

and a yardstick. Here's my advice on the items that I prefer.

- **Bristolboard** This is a thick, firm cardboard. If I plan to use a shape over and over, I draw it on Bristolboard, and then cut it out. (For more on creating these shapes, called templates, see Chapter Three.) Traditionally, rug hookers have used butcher paper to make patterns and templates. That's still a good idea, although the paper shapes won't last as long as ones that are cut from Bristolboard.

- **Charcoal** I don't use charcoal much because it's messy. I prefer to sketch on burlap with markers, usually using pencils in my sketch-books, yet charcoal is good to have on hand. I sometimes play with it while drawing people with clothes when I'm trying to capture the folds in the fabric. I can get the effect that I want by turning the charcoal on its side and swiping it along the paper.

- **Markers** Like many rug hookers, I prefer the black, fine-line Sharpie brand. This type is indelible and permanent. I have used other markers, but they aren't as good—a year

## East Coast Framing Tradition

I like to hook at a table frame, so-called because the frame itself is a table. My favorite is called a Cheticamp. It's named after a small community on Cape Breton, Canada's East Coast. The frames are handmade, often by the husbands of the Cheticamp rug hookers. Residents of Cheticamp traditionally made rugs from yarn, but that didn't stop me from trying their style of frame. Once I tried it, I was hooked and now sell them from my studio.

The beauty of a table frame is that you can lay your wool, scissors, and hook, right on the frame. You don't have to balance the frame on your knees while you hook, your hands are free to make the rug. I like to say that women used table frames for the last 150 years because they were comfortable, not because they hadn't thought of lap frames.

The Cheticamp is very wide (mine is 80"), but narrow. I place the backing over the frame, wrap the backing around the horizontal bars, and then quickly sew the backing to a piece of canvas that is attached to the roller bars of the frame. I always use upholstery thread for this because it is very strong

and won't break. Believe me, my stitching isn't very fancy. To make the backing nice and taut, I turn a gear on the side of the frame.

It's important to design and hook in a place where you feel comfortable and relaxed. Set up a place for yourself. It doesn't have to be a full studio. Use whatever space you have, even if it's a corner of your living room. Choose a good chair, lighting, and music. Think about where you'll store your wool. Make this a place you want to be.

later, I'll find that the lines that I drew on burlap have bled or faded.

- **Pen** Whether you're making a journal entry or sketching, there's a lot of pleasure doing so with a good pen. Go to a shop that lets you try different brands. Experiment before buying. If you enjoy the way that a pen works, you'll look forward to using it. When I buy a new pen, I always feel like a kid opening a fresh, new book at the start of a school year.

- **Pencils** I use Staedtler pencils. An entire set is wonderful, but not necessary. Start out with a 2B and 4B. The numbers refer to the lead weight, or thickness. As you sketch more and more, you'll discover that different lead weights give you different results. In my studio you'll find thicker leads on hand, like 5B, 6B, 7B, and 8B. The higher the number, the wider and darker the line you'll get when you draw. By changing pencils, you won't have to press hard or make multiple lines with a single thickness of one weight.

- **Scissors** I always use scissors with 5 $^1/_2$" blades. These are the best for hand cutting wool. I roll up a length of wool and then cut through the layers to get a wool strip. You can also fold the wool accordian style and cut it into strips this way. It's much quicker than cutting one long strip at a time. When I splurge on a new pair of scissors—for a whopping $3—I write my name and the date on them. This shiny new set becomes my wool scissors and I only use them for wool—nothing else. They won't stay sharp if you cut burlap or paper with them. My old wool scissors are demoted to cutting Bristolboard and paper.

- **Sketch-books** These are essential for designing. Get several that aren't fancy. I like the coil-bound type because tucking a leaf or other treasure between the pages won't damage the binding, and I can flip it open to expose a whole page. I also pick up cheap hardbound versions that I find at dollar stores. These are the ones that I tuck here, there, and everywhere.

- **T-square** Want an easy way to draw perfect corners on your borders? Use a T-square. It will give you a nice, 2" wide guide that's perfect for a 2", 4", or 6" wide versions.

- **Yardstick** Get a metal one, because wood often bows. You'll use the yardstick all the time for drawing straight lines.

- **Yarn** The most glorious colors are tucked into baskets and hung on walls and doors throughout my studio. I like to hook really heavy or really thin yarn strands into my rugs.

Remember the fearless days of your youth? As children we didn't have a problem picking up a crayon and were proud of our drawing, and loved it when our work ended up on the refrigerator door. I admire the way that my daughter, shown in this photo, took to designing. When she feels like hooking, she often sketches directly on the burlap, and then pulls out her wool and hook and starts to play. Sometimes she consults with me about color choices, but that's about the limit of my input.

How many times have you heard someone say, "I can't draw"? Whenever I hear this, I always think of a favorite quote from Pablo Picasso, "Every child is an artist. The problem is how to remain an artist once he grows up."

When you're drawing for rug hooking, you're not trying to create a fine sketch to frame and hang on a wall. Your sketch isn't the end of the line. If it doesn't look quite right, you can change it when you draw it on a backing. You can change any part of it when you're hooking. Even when you've finished the mat, you can still go back, pull out some loops, and rework a section.

People have built-in blocks about design. They've decided that they can't draw and that, without this skill, they're incapable of designing a rug. This just isn't so. I'm proof of this, because I stopped drawing for many years. When I was in grade two, I noticed that my cousin drew excellent pictures. I thought, "I can't draw very well, so why bother?" A lot of people are intimidated by the abilities they see in others. Don't compare yourself to others, and don't be too critical of your own work. It was only when I started rug hooking that I again picked up a pencil and sketch-book

Drawing isn't a necessary part of design. You can have a great idea and get someone else to draw it for you. But I encourage everyone to overcome the fear because drawing will help you create great designs, as well as record ideas and images.

Part of the fear that some rug hookers have about design is from their past experiences. They have been taught through strict methods and have learned to do very specific things with patterns. They think designs should be perfect. Good design means that the work is pleasing to the viewer. The viewer isn't searching for flaws. In fact, the most highly prized rugs at auctions are the very simple designs, the ones

**Oak Leaves Table Mat,** 12" x 24", #6- and #8-cut wool on burlap, Designed and hooked by Deanne Fitzpatrick, Amherst, Nova Scotia, Canada, 2004.

that women created in their homes by drawing on burlap with a piece of charcoal. Primitive rug hooking is about filling in an outline.

Your first rug design can be something really simple. If you think you can't draw anything at all, make a heart. You can do this shape freehand or else trace a valentine. Or what about tracing family feet for a doormat? Stripes are fun and easy. Anyone can draw lines. Whatever you decide to trace or draw . . . do it! Do anything that will get you over the hump.

Sketching designs isn't an instant process. Be willing to risk your time and waste a day. Play around with your ideas and don't expect your work to be perfect. Your final design might be cobbled together from bits and pieces that you sketched throughout the day. You might even find something discarded earlier looks great when you look back on it with a less critical eye. I've often found that a mistake has been the best thing that could have happened. Sometimes a line in the wrong place, or a design that is a bit off balance gains new life by adding a tree in the corner, or a woman in the foreground.

Making a pattern isn't a mystery project. It's about noticing the simplest of things, like an oak leaf, and then taking a second look. You'll discover that you can simplify the shape, boil it down to an outline, and then draw that.

The design I created for the mat shown above, for example, started when a pretty leaf caught my eye outside a hockey arena. I tucked it into a sketch-book. Later, I sketched the shape several times until I liked the result. I used the leaf itself as a template for some of the sketches. Alone, the oak leaf shape is okay, but it turned into an interesting pattern by simply adding a central diamond, rotating, and repeating the leaf shapes, and then adding borders to two sides of the mat.

Your fear will go away if you keep drawing regularly.

Drawing is a technical skill that can be learned. As your skills develop, though, you could be facing other challenges. This is part of the creative process, so embrace it. Take a look at the detail of my rug *Standing Before the Monument*, below. As I hooked, I worried that the snowflakes wouldn't work. I forged ahead anyway, and overcame this fear. The thought of spending nearly two months on a rug that might not work was daunting. It took a good walk, and some time away from the project to forge ahead.

The good thing about hooking rugs is that you can go back to a finished rug and change things that don't look right. Knowing this gives me the confidence to proceed on instinct.

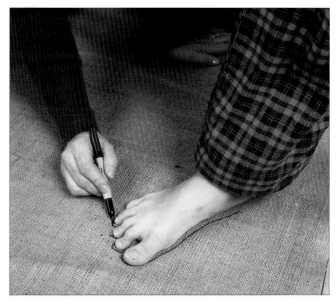

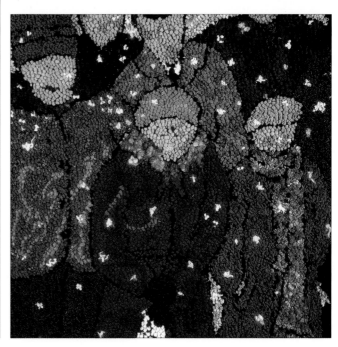

Pens, pencils, and sketch-books are the most basic tools of my trade and they're scattered throughout my studio. If they're left out and easily accessible, I'll use them more. This is important because drawing is a habit that needs to be developed. Like exercise, sometimes you'll only know how good it feels after you do it. That means sometimes you need to sit and draw, even when you don't feel like it. These times may not lead to great inspiration, but they do form a habit.

When I feel as if I have no ideas, these are the times that I realize I've been neglecting my sketch-books. All I have to do to express myself is pick them up. A pencil with a thick lead can fill in an area of a sketch or give me a heavier, darker line on my paper. A swoop down the page with a piece of charcoal instantly looks like a fold in a piece of fabric. Such creativity from simple tools!

The thing that I like to tell people is that I didn't draw before I started hooking. Maybe I did a little doodling, but that's it, since about grade two. That's when I stopped because I thought other people were better than me. This often happens with older children. At first we draw straight from our spirit, without judgement about our skills. We start to evaluate our drawings and become critical of our efforts as we grow up. Then some of us throw down our crayons.

My desire to make authentic East Coast mats is what pulled me back to drawing. I started out wanting my rugs to be as authentic as possible. In this region, people traditionally drew their own patterns. Even if there was a store right in front of me, I still wouldn't have bought a pattern because my grandmother didn't use them for her mats.

Comparing a drawing to someone else's—or believing that you just can't draw—have stopped many rug hookers from making their own designs. Emotional blocks shouldn't stop you. Drawing is a technical thing. It's not a talent but a skill that people learn by practicing. Art is the creation, and your art is rug hooking. Drawing for rug designs is like making pictures that you can later color with crayons.

You don't have to sit perfectly upright at a table when you draw. As you sketch more and more, you'll find your groove. I often end up slouched down in a comfy wingback chair, or else cross-legged on the floor with a sketch-book in my lap. One fall I spent hours sitting in a hockey rink, sketching while my children practiced on the ice. Oh, the

books I filled! I'll never make that many hockey rugs, but I did get some great sketches. I was replicating movement and creating the habit of observing what I saw around me.

When I'm ready to copy a drawing from my sketch-book onto burlap, I sprawl on the floor and copy the image, free-hand, on a larger scale. Even though I'm using a fine-tip indelible felt pen, I don't worry about mistakes. After all, they'll disappear when I hook-in the wool.

## Holding a Pencil

When people come to my workshops, one of the first exercises I have them do is learn to hold a pencil. Sure, we've all been doing this since we were in kindergarten. But I've found that drawing is easier when the pencil is held a certain way, as shown above left. Holding your pencil loosely can make quite a difference in your ability. Hold it loosely, with a gentle grip, like you would the stem of a flower. Now draw lightly and gently.

The worst thing that you can do is grab a pencil (or hook for that matter) and hold it really tightly. Sometimes I can see muscles tensing in the forearms of some students holding a pencil really hard. I want you to try this so that you know what not to do. Draw with the tightly held pencil and take note of how it feels.

## Drawing a Line

So often I've heard the exclamation, "I can't draw a straight line." This is a good thing. Drawing is not about making straight lines. Good heavens, we have rulers to help us do that! Don't decide that your ability to draw should be based on this. In fact, the importance of drawing is *not* being able to draw a straight line. There aren't many straight lines in the world—most are curved and organic. Even a house doesn't have straight lines, unless it's a brand new one that's ship-shape.

I'd like you to get used to the flow of drawing by making a series of gently flowing lines. Some students aren't keen on this exercise. They say, "I'm drawing nothing; what's the sense of this?" I tell them that the first thing they have to do

when they get a new tool is familiarize themselves with it. They need to find out what it can do.

Hold the pencil lightly in your hand and draw a line across a piece of paper, as shown above center. Just as you should hold your pencil lightly, you should also draw lightly. Don't make the mistake of pushing the pencil tip into the paper, denting the surface with the lead. And don't *push* the pencil because that can tear the paper.

Try shading a bit of an area by pressing a little bit harder, or switching to a pencil with a softer, thicker lead.

Now, as shown above right, continue drawing soft, squiggly lines. Pretend that you're making the silhouettes of hillsides completely filling the page. Draw in every direction and play with the way that you hold and move the pencil.

### ▶ TIP  Spoil Yourself

Drawing is about commitment. Get a sketch book that is hard bound and has a coil binding, something that looks like an artist's book, with quality, mid-weight pages. You can draw on anything, but having nice materials will change the way you think about what you draw. It's too easy to toss bits of plain bond sheets in the garbage. You'd lose track of your progess. Sketch-books record your journey. When I look at my earliest sketch-books I realize how far I've come. The first designs I drew were in a lined Hilroy exercise book, the same type that I used to write my ABCs in in kindergarten. I'd scoff at that now. How can you draw pictures in a lined book? I did, and it reminds me of my roots as an artist.

## Learning to See Anew

On the next few pages, I'm going to show and explain some basic drawing skills that will help you get started. But, before that, I'd like to offer some advice.

- **Accept Yourself.** There are many ways of drawing. Don't expect the subjects you sketch to look anything like the same subject drawn by a friend. And don't worry about subjects that give you trouble. Practice at first on the thing that you have some inkling on how it's drawn and keep practicing to help it look better.

    For example, I can't draw beautifully shaded, perfect faces. Instead, I make designs that emphasize what I do well. The people in my rugs have simple faces, yet the way that they pose—and the movement and drape of their clothes—is very distinct, well defined. That's where I excel.

    From time to time, I do try to work on the things that I can't draw, and I encourage you to do the same. I've always had trouble drawing animals. So one summer I sat by a horse barn and did about 20 sketches of a horse that lived there. Eventually, I managed to get a shape that had some semblance of a horse. Of course, when I hooked this rug I really got it right because I work best with hook in hand. Drawing is just the first step.

- **Look critically at rug patterns.** I approached my first design experience with confidence. I had been looking at drawings and rug patterns, and suddenly realized that the designs could be simple and still make a good mat.

Remember, you're basically drawing little outlines.

- **Take back your time.** Even a person with a very full life can find time to draw. If you always have a sketch-book and pen or pencil nearby, you can pull them out whenever there's a free moment. Think about all the little time-stealers in your life: waiting for children, standing in line, riding a bus. How can you put them to good use? Tuck a small sketch-book in your purse and put another in the glove compartment of your car so that your tools are always handy. Commit to the idea that you will sketch.

- **Avoid delays.** When an idea or image pops up, sketch it right away. Don't slow down by trying to get every line just right, first get everything on paper. In many ways, your sketch-book is a visual record of ideas that could turn into a design some day. The important thing is to get a record of the idea. You can work to put the details on later.

- **Draw for the joy of it.** I'm not always sketching to make a design for my next rug. At times, I'm just sketching as an observer. Indirectly, this helps me hone my design skills. I use my sketch-books as reference material. I put the full ones on shelves, as if they're books in a library. A year or two later, when the mood strikes, I leaf through them. Through fresh eyes, the sketches that I once thought were throw-aways often end up looking like they have a lot of design potential.

### Sketching Quickly

Let's say that you're about to draw something for the first time. You have a nice sketch-book in front of you, and your pencil is poised over the paper. Looking at the subject you want to draw, are you wondering, "Where do I begin?"

It's easy to get lost in the details of the thing that you're trying to draw. As you begin to draw, try looking at the subject with a less critical eye. When you put pencil to paper, sketch quickly. Give yourself a time limit of 30 seconds or a minute, and capture only the essential element—be that the outline or feeling of the thing—on paper.

Your goal isn't to get every little detail in the drawing. Instead, you want to make quick lines that capture the form.

1. Give yourself a list of five or six things that you'd like to draw. I'd include a car, bird, flower, house, and tree. You'll be drawing the shapes from your memory of what they look like.

2. Open your sketch-book, grab a pencil and, when you're ready to start, set a timer for 30 seconds, Now draw the first object and give yourself a fresh page for each object. Try to get the entire shape on the paper before the timer sounds. You can sketch with long, sweeping lines or short, quickly overlapping strokes. Do what feels right.

3. Continue making 30-second sketches of the other items on your list.

## Exploring Negative Space

Another way to look at shapes is to not look at them. By this I mean that you look at the shapes around and between objects. You can draw the so-called "negative" space and end up with the outlines of objects.

Learning to see negative space is a great way to understand the size of items in relation to one another, as these relationships are what drawing is all about. If you'd like to give this a try, here's an activity.

1. On a table or desk, set up a simple still-life. It doesn't have to be pretty or grand. You can use a flowerpot, a squash, and a jar, or a few seashells and rocks.
2. Stand or sit back far enough that you can see all of the items in your still-life. Now, without focusing so much on the actual items, draw the shapes that appear between the items. The forms will naturally emerge.

## Drawing People

Some artists have a knack for drawing people, others don't. Whatever group you fall into, keep in mind that you're not trying to make a likeness of someone. You're just practicing making a form.

When I draw people, I try to look at the relationship between parts of the figure. For example, is the person's head a third or half the length of her arm? The good thing about drawing for rug hooking is that your backing has a grid. You can use this to help establish proportions. Or look through a figure book, like *Barron's Anatomy for the Artist*, by David Sanmiguel (Barrons Educational, 2002).

A jointed wood figure that you can pick up at an art store is great for helping you understand how people move. You can bend and pose it to get an idea what looks natural. Here are some other suggestions for you to pick from to draw people.

- **Take a class.** Let a professional artist show you some tricks so you can do your practicing in a structured environment.

- **Practice at meetings.** Whenever you know you're going to have to sit for awhile, take along a sketch-book and draw the person sitting across from you.
- **Pick a partner.** Sit facing another rug hooker and take turns doing one-minute poses while the other sketches. Work really quickly, capturing the essence, like the slant of a shoulder. Don't aim for a likeness of the other person.
- **Join life drawing groups.** In many communities, especially those with art colleges, there are often groups of artists that meet together and hire a nude model so that they can spend a few hours drawing. Drawing nudes is a great way to understand the shape and movement of the human body.
- **Get some books.** There are many books on drawing that offers tons of practice tips and exercises. You can pick out a few from the library to explore, and purchase the one that best suits you. One of the most famous is *Drawing on the Right Side of the Brain*, by Betty Edwards (Penguin/Putnam, 1979, 1989, and 1999).

## Drawing with Your "Wrong" Hand

If you still aren't convinced that you can draw, I have the perfect activity for you to try. It will prove that you have more ability than you think.

1. Sit at a table with a piece of paper in front of you.
2. Pick up a pencil with your non-dominant hand. In other words, if you write with your right hand, hold the pencil in your left hand.
3. Using your non-dominant hand, draw a simple flower on the paper. Note how little control you have over your hand. It's probably quite ineffective, nevertheless, you can still capture the form of the flower. When you put the pencil back in your dominant hand you will realize just how much ability you actually have.

## CHAPTER TWO

# Original Design Plan

There's a beautiful, big tree outside my home, right next to my rug hooking studio. My kids love it because there's a limb that's the perfect height—and strong enough—to support a swing. I always loved the tree, but it wasn't until I saw this photo that I realized what a striking silhouette it had. To use the shape, I'd simplify it by capturing only the sweep of the limbs, which have been shaped by the direction that the wind usually blows. I wouldn't try to draw every twig. The tree would also be great inspiration for an abstract design that captures the wild intertwining of the limbs.

This tree is a perfect example of how we should keep our eyes open to design possibilities. Inspiration is inside us and all around us. Our emotions, environment, and personal history can lead to some powerful images.

In this chapter, I'm going to explain how I come up with my rug designs. These experiences, and some exercises, which I call activities, will, I hope, give you some insight into the creative process.

I have always been in the habit of putting small pockets of inspiration around the house. I'll set my collection of wooden crows above the piano, bits of wood on a shelf in the pantry, postcards between the pages of my journals and sketch books, and seashells on the window ledge in the bathroom. As I gathered objects in preparation for the photo shoot for this book, I put them all together on a little shelf in my office. The effect was so warm. It was like I gathered all these loose thoughts together and laid them on a blanket. They belonged together because they were related to one another in all kinds of different ways.

This was a good activity. You might want to gather up bits of your life that you've been saving, and view them like the page of a scrapbook. It will surely lead to inspiration.

The starting point for inspiration is looking at the world around you, and I mean *really* looking. Do you notice the houses that you drive past every day? Do you look at the way your mother or close friend always carries her purse? I guess what I'm asking you to do is stop and see—as well as smell—the roses. Your mind needs to be at work creating a visual diary of the world around you.

Collect ideas, inspiration, and shapes. I can't offer you a timeline, or write down steps, but I can tell you what works.

The advice that follows—in fact, this entire book—is just such a gentle guide. Essentially, I'd like you to start thinking about your beliefs, ideas, personal sources of inspiration, and values.

- **Surround yourself with beauty.** Buy art. Read good books. Go to art galleries. Visit studios. Talk to other artists. Join a rug hooking or creativity group that nourishes you. Decide that you're on the lookout for design ideas. When you make this a conscious effort, design ideas will emerge.

- **Trust yourself.** Above all else, take everything that you see and learn with a grain of salt. Don't create a lot of rules for yourself based on the teachings of others. Be cautious. Trust your intuition. Exercise and develop your own sense of balance and color by finishing rugs.
- **Get to know yourself.** Look at the world with all of your senses. Pay attention to your visual responses to the room you're in, or the field that you're walking through. Smell, touch, taste, hear, and look at the world around you.

  This is more important than you might at first think. Have you ever compared the way that you hook when you're watching television, when it's quiet, and when you're listening to fiddle music? The rhythm of your fingers varies, so your loops probably look a bit different. Your color choices might not be the same. Your emotions affect the way that you hook a rug, so it makes sense that your feelings about your environment will affect the designs that you create.
- **Look for emotional connections.** The other day I was coming down the stairs from the second floor of my studio and I realized that I was thinking about my mother. In my mind's eye, I was seeing her on her knees, mopping up water that had leaked into the house during a rainstorm. Our kitchen and living room were on the first floor, and there were leaks.

  This was a powerful image because I had an emotional connection. It was about more than my mother mopping, it reflected her relationship with both me and my father. I immediately roughed some drawings in one of my many sketch-books. What started out as a thought-provoking idea turned into a sketch that might turn into something more . . . some day.
- **Sketch everything.** Like I've said before, you don't have to be able to draw to record your ideas. If an image strikes your fancy, draw stick men. The key is to get all of the elements onto the page, in a relationship that you think works. At this point, just get something down so that you can hang on to the idea. Sketch it roughly, just enough to remind you of the visual idea you had in your head.

- **Start journaling.** Jot down ideas as they come to you. I've come up with ideas when walking, swimming, doing anything that is repetitive enough to become meditative. This will happen more and more as you get in touch with yourself. Don't count on remembering even the simple ideas. You'll lose them. When I look back through my journals, I discover designs that I didn't even realize I had!

  I think of my journals and sketch books as a record of my life and what I was thinking and feeling at particular times. This is a good place to write down the stories that make up your life.
- **Create an inspiration book, drawer, or shelf.** My sketchbooks do triple duty. In any one, you'll find journal entries and drawings, plus small treasures tucked between the pages. You never know what will become a source of inspiration. Collect anything that catches your eye.
- **Find out what you like.** Really start thinking about what you like when you admire something. When you walk into a room or a gallery and you are drawn to an object try to take notes about what aspects of the object are attracting you. Is it the color? The shape? The silhouette? Only by knowing what you like can you trust your intuition.

I own a great bit of property just a short drive from my house. It's a flat stretch of land that slopes down at the back to reveal the Bay of Fundy. The neighbors there must think I'm crazy, because every once in a while I go up and sit on the land, enjoying the view. This has become quiet time for me.

This restful time, as well as my walks in the woods, got me thinking about the way that nature changes through the seasons.

How has this idea become a rug? The trick was turning the concept into a design. I ended up creating a series of rugs that shows how fields change, how the colors of early October are different from early November. I paid close attention to colors as the seasons changed, as well as sketched a lot. This example shows how embracing inspiration can lead to a concept.

An image popped into my mind once, and I have been holding on to it for some time. I see a man running through the night with a fiddle on his back. I'm not sure that I have every tool, technically, to deliver that image in a rug design yet. I may not be able to capture the man's motion and this means I will have to sketch and resketch. I will have to watch boys running with their skates on their backs and imagine that the skates are fiddles. I have the daily work of an artist to do before this rug comes to fruition. I must watch, and I must sketch.

Once you have an idea, you don't need to act on it right away, as long as you've recorded it somewhere. You won't always be ready at the time that it comes to you. You might be in the middle of another project. You might just have the

## Old Is New

Don't be inhibited by excluding ideas that others have already tried. No one owns the idea of laundry on a line, a trickling brook, a ship sailing the sea, or a starry night. Seek inspiration. Allow yourself to grow from the art of others, because art creates art. There's no need to copy, you need to re-create.

basic sketch, but you don't have a sense of the colors. You could have all of the emotional connections, but you haven't figured out all of the technical details.

The approach I use most often is to mull over an idea. I'll write about it. I'll list everything that I can about the idea. What I'm trying to do is work it out so completely that I

## Listing Elements

**B**ased on what I've explained already, here's a step-by-step guide that I offer students at my workshops. It's an easy way to help you sort out what's really important and belongs in the design that you're developing.

1. Write down all of the elements (both ideas and things) that come to mind when you think about the idea or subject of your rug.
2. Organize the list of elements in order of importance. If some things are equally important, place them side-by-side.
3. Choose only the most important elements for your rug. You don't need to put everything into one design. You want the finished rug to express the essence of your idea.

have a thorough understanding of it. Then, finally, I reduce the idea to the most important elements, which will become the start of the design.

Let's say that you want to design and hook an original rug that honors friendship between women. First, write down all of the things that you associate with this concept. I think about warmth, shared activities, and celebrating relationships.

The next step is narrowing down your list to items that you can sketch. I've always associated friendship with sharing bread, so I sketched a woman with a loaf of bread in her hands. This led to a sketch of a group of women making bread. (See the photo above right.) It's important to sketch an idea several different ways, so that you find something that really speaks to you. Two women having tea expresses friendship; so does a group of women dancing. With several sketches, I'm well on my way to developing a friendship rug.

What I won't do is make one rug that includes all of these sketches. I don't want the rug to seem like a grab bag of ideas jumbled together. In fact, this is a common mistake of people who are new to designing. There is a tendency to complicate, rather than simplify. Think about what it is that you're creating, what it is you really want to express. Focus on that and nothing else.

From time to time, a hooker will tell me that she wants to make a rug for her husband. She'll want to make an original design that shows the things he loves. When we get to the exercise where we make a list, it's a mile long. At this point, we narrow down the subject to one item, like the family cottage. The next thing I know, the hooker has sketched a cottage that includes their boat, fishing gear, three children, and a dock for the boat. That's enough content for five rugs.

Another common mistake that people make is putting all of the extra items into the border, where they become disconnected icons floating on a color background. There's nothing wrong with this approach when your rug is about expressing love. But if you're interested in good design, it isn't the right way to go.

At left, you can see how I handled a cottage theme rug, distilling it to its most important elements.

**The Harrison Cottage,** 30" x 24"; #6-, #8-, and hand-cut wool on burlap; Designed and hooked by Deanne Fitzpatrick, Amherst, Nova Scotia, Canada, 2004.

**Getting the Rural Mail,** 48" x 64", #6- and #8-cut wool on burlap. Designed and hooked by Deanne Fitzpatrick, Amherst, Nova Scotia, Canada, 2004. This mat is a good example of how an idea can be expressed in a rug. I believe that part of enjoying life is realizing how close I actually am to death. I don't think of this in a morbid way, but in a realistic, practical way. To show this in a mat, I came up with the main theme, that there is beauty in daily activities and I should appreciate the simple things in life. This didn't give me any shapes that I could draw on burlap. Like I have encouraged you to do, I had to think through the theme more completely. I realized that when I am at my best, I appreciate waving at my neighbor as I go out to my broken-down mailbox to see what has arrived. This was something I could work with. A graveyard became the symbol for the closeness of death, and how near it is even when we're enjoying socializing with our neighbors. You can learn more about this rug in "The Gallery."

I was lucky to live in a family—and a community—that loved to share stories. If you listen closely to those around you, you'll probably discover that there are plenty of tales in your own home that you can gather for a rug.

My father, bless his soul, was an amazing storyteller. People who visited "from away" enjoyed seeing him because he made them feel they were home again. In the time since my parents' death I've realized that many of the stories I tell in my mats are ones that I learned from them. I never hauled a net from the rough Atlantic waters, nor salted a fish for market, but I watched those things being done, and remembered what was said.

Listening is about really hearing what the other person is telling you. You do it best when you aren't waiting to intervene with a story of your own. The best stories are heard when you are right there, fully aware that you need to be quiet and take it in.

**New Year's Eve in St John's Harbour,** 62" x 30", #6- and #8-cut wool on burlap. Designed and hooked by Deanne Fitzpatrick, Amherst, Nova Scotia, Canada, 1993. From the collection of Joan Beswick.

Children are great listeners . . . when they want to hear what parents are talking about in another room. It's never too late to rediscover this childlike-skill. Rather, it's in the domain of anyone willing to stop and take it all in.

It's important to keep a record of what you hear and jot down your stories in a journal. Recently, Jim Reilly, a man in his mid-70s, came from town to clean up the abandoned farm equipment around my yard. He was up at dawn, strong as an ox, cutting apart the metal and loading it onto his truck. At lunch I invited him in for a little stewed chicken. In the sunshine of my kitchen, he talked about being an African American growing up in Amherst, about wild rides through Victoria Street with chickens flying off the back of a truck and training for an Olympic boxing team. The things I never knew and the mats I could make. I wrote his story down right away.

Stories are out there waiting to be told, wanting to be collected. As you listen to the stories of your friends and family, share your own. This is good for your heart and, in the telling, you'll hone skills that will help you summarize a story in a way that will create a beautiful mat. *Writing Down the Bones* by Natalie Goldberg (Shambhala Publications, 1986) is a good book for people who want to sort out their stories.

Don't worry about being too literal. For years, my father sat on the edge of my bed and explained why we didn't have

## Story Time

You have to decide that your stories are worth sharing. They do have value, but it takes a strong sense of self to come to this conclusion. So, sometimes, the work on your story rugs start with developing confidence. At first, just share your experiences and story rug designs with a few people. When you feel their positive responses you'll feel better about sharing with even more people.

To get started, take 10 minutes and write down everything you can possibly think of that's a story you might turn into a hooked rug. Briefly jot down the event, person, and idea in a list format. Don't stop to evaluate any story's worth as a rug, just get it down as a possibility. You can enhance the stories on your list later. Time yourself and write, write, write for 10 minutes.

old photos or much family memorabilia. He said that before I was born, his mother and father were moving from their outport by dory. All the stuff they were bringing was loaded into the boat. But there were one too many boxes, the boat tipped, and everything was lost in the water.

Years later, when I recounted this to my uncle he said he never heard of any such thing happening. Whether it was true or not, I don't know, but I do have a visual image of the possessions of a lifetime falling overboard. The truth was probably that most of the family pictures we did have were lost when our house caught fire and burned to the ground before I was born.

One of the things I learned from my father is that the best part of a story isn't always the truth. Sometimes he would add a little flavor. A story is just a story, and your goal is to make it as interesting as possible. Likewise, it sometimes takes a little enhancing to make a great mat. Tell the truth as beautifully as you can, but don't sacrifice beauty for truth. If a field of goldenrod that you're hooking needs a little lavender, add it.

Where I grew up in Freshwater, most of the houses were white clapboard. My rugs often show villages similar to my childhood home, but the houses in my rugs are very colorful, just like the stories and the people. As the rug on page 22 shows, what I'm after is a good rug. I'm willing to sacrifice the truth for what is good for the eye.

Family pictures are a great place to look for stories. I'm still working on the design that I want to base on the old photo of the little girl shown on page 22. That's me! I have such warm feelings about the photo, because I'm wearing my very first dress. I love the pose and the image has a lot of potential for a rug. There's so much that I could do with the background and imagine the fun I could have playing with colors and textures for the sky and field.

Get your albums out with the black-and-white photos which are a great source for stories. It doesn't matter if you have all of the details, just pay attention to the feelings and memories that the images evoke.

When I look at an old photograph, I always wonder about the circumstances beyond the edges of the picture, the parts that I can't see. Who took the picture? Why was it taken? What lies behind the picture? What is the person thinking about? Asking yourself these questions are great for the imagination, especially if you are not worried about the truth, because most of these questions can't be answered factually. The picture, just like a good pictorial mat, gets the mind going and the viewer is only given a hint of the real story.

A great way to come up with a picture rug is to explore the events in your own life. Remember the life line activity

## Telling Your Story

Here's an exercise that you can do with a friend. I learned about it at a goal setting for women in business workshop I attended with Ella McQuinn, of McQuinn and Company (a marketing and business coaching company). I have adapted it so that it can be helpful to people who want to develop an idea into a rug.

1. For five minutes,(use a timer) sit with a friend and talk, uninterrupted, about an idea or story that you have for a mat. Say everything you can, let the words flow freely, without holding anything back.

2. Turn the table, and give your friend the same gift. Listen intently for five minutes as she talks about the idea or story she has for her mat. You both will find that it is a rare thing to be able to speak freely and uninterrupted for five minutes with out feeling guilty or boring or any number of other things.

3. Now it's time to discuss what you heard and "saw" in each other's ideas and stories. Sometimes this free flow of ideas leads to great idea for images that you can hook into a mat.

**Hockey Night In Nova Scotia,** 32" x 34", #6- and #8-cut wool on burlap. Designed and hooked by Deanne Fitzpatrick, Amherst, Nova Scotia, Canada, 2003.

that I had you do back on page 18? Some people think that very little they've seen or done is worthwhile. How wrong that is. You have so much to bring to your mats.

Once you have an idea or story—and honed-in on a main theme—just how do you turn this into a rug? Let's say that I want to make a rug that shows my son's reaction when the weather turns really cold. My family is thrilled, because it means that we can start making the backyard rink. But how can I show cold, cold weather and mounds of snow without some people interpreting the rug as depressing, or reminding them how much they hate winter.

Showing emotion in rugs isn't an easy thing to do. The old adage, "A picture paints a thousand words" is true enough, but just how does it do that? Consider your color choices.

Bright colors are cheerful. Look at a detail of *Hockey Night in Nova Scotia*, above. The snow sparkles a little because I hooked in a smidge of glittery fiber. This is a night scene, yet the dark sky doesn't feel oppressive. It seems illuminated and very active. There's also joy here in the movement, the tilt of the head, and the action.

The way that you show people in a rug can also portray emotion. The type of clothing they're wearing, for example, can tell a bit of the story, and lead the viewer to think about them in a certain way. It's pretty easy to tell that the kids in my hockey rug love what they're doing.

Once you make your rug design, step back and assess it. You don't want the story and the content to be so defined that people can't interpret it themselves. Leave enough unsaid that someone looking at the finished rug will see other things in it. A rug should be emotive. Some will think exactly what you had in mind, others will be moved in an entirely different way. A good rug and a good image will evoke many stories other than your own.

In my kitchen hangs a rug called *Grace Mercy and Peace*,

**Grace Mercy and Peace,** 32" x 36", #6- and #8-cut wool on burlap, Designed and hooked by Deanne Fitzpatrick, Amherst, Nova Scotia, Canada, 2000.

shown at right. When the door leading from the kitchen to the studio is open, people look in and see the rug. They often ask what it means. Instead of giving my view, I ask them what they think the image expresses. Some think it's sad, others think the woman has just enjoyed a delicious meal. Others believe she is praying. I have had people chuckle at the rug, while others hang their head. I love the mystery and appreciate each response because it is personal. It would be much harder if they just walked by unaffected by what I believe to be a rug full of energy and emotion.

Remember that the border can also be part of the story. It's a great place to write a message, set down a date or place, or repeat a motif or symbol that's important to the story. That's what I did when I created *Standing Before the Monument*. The photo at right is a detail of the rug, which is shown in its entirety on page 69. The rug shows a group of women commemorating a terrible explosion that leveled much of Halifax. But it was not the historic event that inspired me—I was thinking about the women approaching the end of their lives, and reflecting upon it. Thus, in the border I wrote, "Unlike the poet, my life has most often taken the road well traveled and I have made it whole with gifts of bread to neighbors." It's my belief that most of us have no great happening to mark our time on earth. We're traced by small gifts, warm embraces, decency, and goodness. This rug for me is as much about my beliefs and values as it is about the Halifax explosion.

If you include a message, don't write what's already in the rug. For example, if the rug portrays a wedding, you don't have to write "David and Sylvia, 1996." Instead, include a little poem or a comment about caring and love.

The wool you use can also be part of the story of the rug. The winter after my mother died, I took apart her green wool car coat and used it to sign my initials in many of the rugs I made thereafter. The coat still smelled of her.

The title of the rug tells a lot about the story. Always look for a good title. Titling your rug is probably the simplest and most effective way of making a point. Calling a rug *Cat #3* is fine, but it tells us little about the cat. You need to describe some things about the cat in the title. For example who owns the cat? What is it doing? Where is it? The title is a chance to describe what you would like to say.

## CHAPTER THREE

# Designing with Templates

Templates are a time-honored tradition. They're as much a part of rug hooking as stamped backs (patterns drawn or stenciled onto burlap). At the turn of the century, and perhaps even before, women carefully saved the brown paper that store-bought goods were wrapped in. This paper became templates for mats. Women would copy the design off a favorite china cup, or copy the rose on the stamped pattern bought from a door-to-door peddler. The paper template was traced in different ways, to create patterns for mats that warmed the parlor or greeted back-door visitors.

The rugs shown in the photo at right have great variety, yet they were created from only two handfuls of templates. I cut out the basic shapes, and then moved them around on my burlap until I liked the arrangement. In some cases, I decided to enlarge or reduce the templates to get the look that I wanted. Once I was happy, I traced the templates on the backing. Then I added lines, geometric shapes . . . all sorts of fun things to bring each pattern to life.

Cut-outs and stencils, called templates, take much of the fear out of the designing process. Templates aren't a new idea. They've long been used for making patterns for rugs, quilts, and other handicrafts. Even if you use very simple shapes, the rugs that you create can be beautiful, even complex.

All of the rug patterns on the previous page were created using only 10 templates: a crow, a posy-style circle, a star, two houses, two pods, and three leaves. Because I want you to have fun with design, all of these templates are included with this book. Use them freely to recreate the patterns shown in this chapter and, of course, to venture into your own world of design. I sometimes enlarged or reduced the templates 40% to come up with the patterns that are shown in the photo on the previous page. You can reduce or enlarge them as much as you would like. Templates can be adjusted to an unlimited number of sizes and cut apart or added to for even more variety.

The aim of this chapter is drive away any thoughts that designing rugs is frightening. I'm going to lead you to a new level in making rugs by using a set of templates, which are basically a set of simple shapes that you can trace onto a backing. They give you the freedom to design rugs without knowing how to draw, though I know you can draw if you practice.

You can make some great rugs by combining the templates in this book with other simple shapes, such as diamonds and squares, or by adding a border. The templates can be made smaller and used as a border repeat, or enlarged to become a single motif that's the focal point of a rug.

I still like to use templates for scrolls, some animals, and shapes that are often repeated. They're simple forms and they're easy to use. I find some things difficult to draw, so a template is a handy source when I need to make a dog, moose, or whale. Placing or tracing the templates on my backing gives me the opportunity to work out how I want to position some elements without stressing. Art should involve labor (of love), but not be stressed over. Anxiety and tension are not as good for the creative process as books and movies might have us believe. A good artist will work comfortably and freely, going right from the heart and soul onto the backing. Try to relax and have fun.

The templates in *The Secrets of Planning and Designing a Hand-Hooked Rug* are protected by copyright, to prevent

their use for resale. However, they can be used over and over again for your personal use. Please work with them and enjoy them as you create rugs for your home and gifts for loved ones.

I hope that by the time you finish working through this chapter, you'll branch out to make some of your own templates. Better still, start right away and add a few of your own to my collection. What are the one or two things that you can draw well already? Make them into templates.

If you would like to create one of the designs in the finished rugs that are shown in this chapter, all you have to do is cut out your templates, place them on a backing in the same format as the design you have chosen, and then trace shapes with a permanent black marker. Now draw any extra lines that you see, to complete the pattern. Once you do this, you'll have your own stamped pattern. Here's the step-by-step process.

> ▶ **TIP  Play Time**
>
> If you have a hard time visualizing what you might want to use for a rug pattern, play with your templates. Make them big or tiny. Cut them in half. Cut out about eight or ten in all different sizes. Place every one on a backing—together or singly—so that you can see how they'll look. This exercise is sure to give you some ideas about what you want to do.

1 The simplest method for working with the templates in this book is to cut them out and use them exactly as they are. To keep your original patterns in good condition for future use, you might want to work with copies. I traced the templates onto stiff cardboard. But you can use clear plastic, red dot tracer, or another firm material. You can also photocopy the shapes onto clear transparency film (sheets for overhead projectors). It's really easy to cut a template out of the thin sheet foam or bristol board that's sold in craft stores. The down side is that sheet foam is so flexible that it isn't quite as easy to work with on a framed backing.

2 Using these templates is meant to be an exercise for your imagination. Play with your templates. Copy them. Cut some in half. Use a portion of one of the houses on the edge of a mat. Change the doors and windows of a house, add extra trim, or put crisscrosses on the roof. Turn the simple house into a shed or even a church. If you'd like to make a bigger rug, enlarge the designs on a photocopier, and then cut them out. Imagination is all that it takes.

3 To create your own design, begin by placing templates directly on a burlap backing. Move them around to create different designs. When you're happy with the positions, trace the shapes. People have fears about doing this, but it's the very first step in basic design. Another option is to take a large piece of paper and actually use the templates to trace a design on paper before you begin drawing on your burlap. This way you can experiment a little more before you commit yourself. If you feel threatened about tracing, just remember that you can turn the burlap over and start again.

4 Trace your shapes on burlap with a fine-line, indelible felt pen. I like the Sharpie brand. Using a red marker and a black marker helps me distinguish between what is in the foreground and what is in the background. I use the red felt for shapes that will be in the foreground. Once again, don't worry about mistakes, as you can turn over your backing and use the other side. This gives you a second chance right at the start. Rug hooking is a forgiving craft.

**Seven for a Secret Never Told,** 34" x 20", #6- and #8-cut on burlap. Designed and hooked by Deanne Fitzpatrick, Amherst, Nova Scotia, Canada, 2004. A template turns into a pattern when two or more elements are combined. Sure, I've used more than a few templates all by themselves. One of the house templates, for example, hooks up as a great mug mat. My goal with this mat was to express an idea, but that doesn't mean there couldn't be beauty in the design. The crows aren't lined up across a flat background. Instead, I set up an asymmetrical arrangement, so that some are looking in different directions and break into the border. The easiest way to plan a nice arrangement is to photocopy the template the number of times that you want to see it on the mat, and then play with the arrangement of the shapes.

Repeating the star template just a few times added to the arrangement without pulling too much attention away from the birds. I added eyes and lines for wings on the crows. The border is so simple: just some squiggly lines on a green background. So, you're looking at a pattern that's just two templates—a rectangle for the inner edge of the border, and some hand-drawn squiggles.

Using a basic shape doesn't always mean that the rug you create with it is going to be simple, or lacking in meaning. You can add a border, use a second template, or even choose a template with a shape that's full of symbolism. You can also use the border to write a few lines in. Sometimes the simplest things have the greatest of meaning. Think of a gold wedding band. It's really nothing more than a circle, but it evokes many feelings and ideas.

A crow has tremendous meaning to me. I grew up listening to my mother recite a poem about this bird from *Fish and Brewis, Toutens and Tales* by Len Margaret (Breakwater Books, St. John's, Newfoundland and Labrador, Canada, 1980), and the shape always reminds me of her and of life (see the poem, right). I include them because they remind me of my roots. I can still hear my mother counting crows every day. We would get in the car for a Sunday drive, and she would forecast her day by the number of birds she saw on the road as we headed out to the highway. A black bird is a theme I repeat time and time again in my rugs.

## Seven Crows

*One for sorrow,*
*Two for joy,*
*Three for a wedding,*
*Four for a boy,*
*Five for silver,*
*Six for gold,*
*Seven for a secret never told*

When people see the rugs they may see them as just crows, but when I make the rugs I perceive the birds as full of content. They're a warm reminder of my childhood.

**Leaves Falling and Crows,** 18" x 50", #6- and #8-cut wool on burlap. Designed and hooked by Deanne Fitzpatrick, Amherst, Nova Scotia, Canada, 2004.

Note how I'm using the same crow shape in *Leaves Falling and Crows*, above, yet the rug looks so very different from *Seven for a Secret Never Told* on page 28. In this rug, I added basic leaf shapes, rotating them as if they're tumbling to the ground. Don't be afraid to use different colors, or draw in details. When you repeat a template shape, turn it backward, upside down, or tilt it on a slant to give it a unique look.

After I'm happy with the way that my templates are traced on burlap, I start thinking about ways to jazz up the background and the border. One of my favorite tricks is to draw a wide border that cuts through one or more of the shapes that I've drawn on the burlap (see page 41 for more information).

The background behind the templates is a great place to focus your attention. On primitive style mats I never hook straight across in a single color. This will flatten out and dull your artistic efforts. Hook the background in circles, swirls, and even diamonds (see *Little Black Dress* on page 66). Use several similar colors one solid color. Try hooking in a fine silk yarn in curlicues to give the background some extra dimension. When

**Hit and Miss Star,** 30" x 18", #6- and #8-cut wool on burlap. Designed and hooked by Deanne Fitzpatrick, Amherst, Nova Scotia, Canada, 2004.

I say jazz it up, I am talking freestyle and experimental.

Taking one template and repeating it to create a mat will work. Try repeating the same house template four or five times to create a simple door topper. Instead of making it straight across the top edge of the mat, draw a gently curving line and create hills behind the houses.

Color can transform a template. Those houses can be all one color, or each one can be a different. Statements can be made with color. If all of the houses are the same, this says "company houses" while the many colors say "individuals live here."

A simple color change can turn a crow into a seagull or a redbird. Leaves can show the viewer that it's midsummer, or they can indicate that it's autumn. When you use templates there's a lot of room left to express yourself, and develop a vision of the rug you're creating.

Another way that you can play with templates is to create activity in the background. Take a look at *Hit-and-Miss Star* above. What could be easier than arranging stars around the edges of a mat, then placing a couple of larger ones in the center? Lines hooked in hit-and-miss really add sparkle. Hit-and-miss means you take whatever leftover strips you have, put them in a basket, and pull them out randomly for hooking. This type of border can be hooked in stripes, small squares, higgledy-piggledy, or in circular motions. Hit-and-miss is also good when you give some consideration to the colors that you throw in the bag. I like to have a somewhat planned style for the rugs when I'm aiming for an antique look. I will draw out the colors in the body of the rug, and add a few more dull colors to enrich the color palette a bit.

## Exploring the Possibilities

A good template is a valuable tool. One good motif can be used a thousand times in a thousand different ways. It's a theme that can be worked on and developed. As you grow in your artistic ability it will grow with you because you will be able to approach it more creatively all the time.

Using templates is nothing to be ashamed of. If you had a hammer would you use a shoe to pound a nail? Play with your templates as if you're a child with a new Spirograph. You just need to give it permission to play.

1. Choose one template. If necessary, enlarge or reduce it on a photocopier so that it's smaller than a page in your sketch-book.

2. Sketch as many different designs from it as you can in your sketch-book. You don't have to hook anything. Just use this as a design exercise, so that you can get an idea of the range of designs that can be created with one template.

**Little Coral House,** 7" x 7", #6- and #8-cut, wool on burlap. Designed and hooked by Deanne Fitzpatrick, Amherst, Nova Scotia, Canada, 2004. My house template, which I turned into the mat shown above, is based on a gabled house that I like. This building, which is shown in the photo below, is on a farm that's just up the road from my studio that I've walked past for many years. The original house has the same form and some interior lines that are on the template, but a lot of the details on this farmhouse just weren't needed. This doesn't mean I might not add some of them to a future pattern. But, for now, I just used the form and the lines that were most appealing to me.

As soon as I started creating templates, I really began to look at the shape of things. I started seeing forms that are one of the really important things in art. If you can get the form down right, the design will clearly express itself. I began examining objects around me, so that I could pick out the lines that created each form.

Simplifying objects down to their basic lines looks so easy but it does take some practice, and often quite a few revisions. This is the only hurdle you have to get over to start making your own templates. Look through books on artists for simple sketches that are very representative.

I recently visited an exhibit of works by the famous sculptor August Rodin, at The Art Gallery of Nova Scotia. When I walked into the room full of massive bronze sculptures the emotion I felt was all from the forms he had created. At the end of the exhibit were his sketches of nudes. These, too, were about form with the nude created out of a small group of lightly penciled lines. I left the gallery with

two little postcards of nudes to pin up in my office. They'll be inspiration and remind me of what I saw.

You'll never know where your next template will come from. Sometimes you see it in a painting, sometimes you see it on your own, but you'll never see it if you aren't looking for

**Oak Leaf,** 14" x 14", #6- and #8-cut, wool on burlap. Designed and hooked by Deanne Fitzpatrick, Amherst, Nova Scotia, Canada, 2004.

**Flower Pot,** 24" x 14", #6- and #8-cut, wool on burlap.  Designed and hooked by Deanne Fitzpatrick, Amherst, Nova Scotia, Canada, 2004.

it. A good starting point is looking through your sketch-book, to see what you've already created.

To make your first template without resorting to a sketch you've already made, pick a basic shape, like a boat, fish, or house. It helps if you have the object in front of you, for reference. First draw the outline of the shape.

The easiest shape is a leaf, because you can trace the outline directly on to paper. The oak leaf that's in the set of templates with this book, is the result of a happy find. I based it on a leaf that I found outside the new hockey rink in Springhill, Nova Scotia, while on the way to my son's prac-tice. I simply looked above my head and there it hung on a young oak tree. I picked it off, gathered a few more from the ground, and stuck them in a sketch-book that I had handy.

To make the template, all I did was trace around the leaf. You could even trace the leaf right on to your backing. The leaf itself is a template. I had a fun time making it into the *Oak Leaf* rug, shown above.

Look for other objects around the house or yard that might be traceable. Then work your way up to the simple

sketches of slightly more challenging items. With these, your goal is to refine the shape. If you're drawing something large, look at the outside edges (the silhouette) of the shape. What you want to do is simplify the form so that you can re-create it with only a few lines.

I find graphic artists are masters at this. Look at business logos and advertising if you want to learn how you can simplify a complex object. Start with the simplest, pick up a leaf and trace it.

The crow that you see in many of my rugs was inspired by a little crow in a newspaper ad. I tore it out years ago and pasted into (what else?) a sketch-book. I often find little motifs here and there, on a cup, or the back of a book. I use them for inspiration to create shapes of my own. Keep your eyes open and you'll soon have a fine collection of templates to draw upon.

One of the things I like about *Flower Pot*, shown above, is that the flower pot is one of the houses turned upside down. A circle and a star are the flowers, yet that is not what you see when you first look at it. This is a good example of how color, and a few details can transform simple shapes so that the viewer can see something altogether different. The color combination in this rug is one of my favorites. I love the gold, greens, rusts, and taupes that, when combined, remind me of old-time rugs.

## Sharing Your Talents

One of the most delightful design classes I ever gave involved making templates. I found that, in the group, many people were good at drawing different things. I struggle with rendering animals, so one student drew a great whale that I've saved. Another student shared a wonderful little boat template that she created, and so on. With each individual in the class draw-ing the one thing they could do fairly well, we were able to share a beautiful set of templates. The next time your group wants to do something interest-ing, I suggest you create a set of templates for each other. You'll be amazed at the ideas that come out of this. Each member of the group will have a nice memento and it'll be interesting to watch the designs that might emerge in future rugs.

1. Tell them to think about simple shapes they can draw well. Most people have a few doodles that they can do well.

2. Everyone should bring paper, pencils, and a couple of sheets of bristol board.

3. Each member draws a couple of shapes on their bristol board and cuts them out.

4. Pass all of the templates around the room, so that every group member can trace what they want onto their remaining bristol board.

5. In the following weeks challenge each other to sketch some basic designs using the templates. You don't have to hook these unless you want to.

## CHAPTER FOUR

# Practical Methods for Designing

You can sometimes create good designs without paying attention to practical elements, like the balance of shapes and color, focal point, border style and width, and the intended location of a finished mat. Rugs have the grace of being open to a primitive style. But you can create even better rugs when you pay attention to these things, even if your motif is as simple as a star.

The photo on this page features Fish School. This is an overlayed design. A single style of fish is laid over one another and in every possible direction. To compliment the wildness of the fish, I added a a wavy border which further suggests that there is nothing straight about this rug, it is a pool of fish lost in each other and then lost again in the waves. I chose red for the border as a striking contrast to the soft blues of the background sea. I wanted the border to be noticed and to frame up the subtle grays of the fish. A dull colored border in this rug would have given the rug a washed out look. I wanted a "stand up and try to catch me" feeling to the fish.

**The Plant,** 6' x 3', #6- and hand-cut wool on burlap. Designed and hooked by Deanne Fitzpatrick, Amherst, Nova Scotia, Canada, 1995. I like to sprawl on the floor when I'm drawing my designs on burlap. Even though I'm working flat, I always know how the finished mat is going to be viewed because I am picturing it in my head as if it were hanging. If you're drawing a large piece that's going to be a wall hanging, pick it up and put it on the wall every once in awhile. This way, you can see perspective problems as they're developing, rather than after you have completely finished the drawing.

Pictorials should be placed on walls. There's usually a lot of attention to the proportion of things, and they're designed to be viewed from one direction. There's a top and bottom to the rug. If you have a pictorial in your home, place it on the floor and take a look. The perspective will look skewed, and you can't appreciate the image unless you stand right in front of one side of it.

The pictorial shown in this photo works on the floor because it's placed so that it can only be viewed from one direction.

There are basically two different kinds of rugs: ones that are made to hang on a wall, and others that are for the floor. The type that you're creating will affect how you translate your sketches into a composition, what the border will look like and why you'll choose certain hooking materials.

You hover over a floor rug, looking down on it. On the other hand, you look straight at a rug that's hanging on a wall. You can walk right up to it, standing as close as a foot away from the piece. Aside from a rug hooking show, when was the last time you saw someone get down on their hands and knees to examine a floor rug? Floor rugs are usually viewed from no less than five feet away. So when you draw and combine the shapes in your design—the composition—consider how you'll look at the finished rug.

Save your most detailed pictorial designs for where they'll most be appreciated: a mat that's going to hang on a wall. This is also the type of rug that needs the most attention to perspective.

With a floor mat, it doesn't matter if the sizes of different things in the design are in proportion to one another. But be careful what you hook into it so that you don't end up with something that can't go on the floor. It's best to avoid anything

that varies the height of the loops across the surface. You don't want little toes catching in anything. And it would be awful if someone tripped on a raised portion of your work. Consider comfort and wearability. Avoid using a lot of different yarn textures and also fleece in floor mats because it battens down in a different way than cloth does. I still love the patina of the loops of wool cloth once they have been worn in an even, flat way. I generally choose wool cloth strips as the main ingredient for rugs I intend to use on the floor.

You'll have much more freedom with materials when making a mat that will hang on a wall. In fact, pictorials require more dimension to look their best. Hook in bits of hand-cut sweaters, metallic threads, rovings, silk, and yarn. These textures will add dimension and interest that you can't get from using all the same cuts, types, and weights of wool cloth. It is these added textures that allow you to become artful in your approach to rug hooking.

On page 34, there's a detail of my rug *Girl with A Fish*. You can tell that I intended to hang it on a wall. If I placed it on the floor, I'd feel weird walking on the two people. Although the rug is flat, it has visual dimension because the little girl and her fish are standing in front of the older woman.

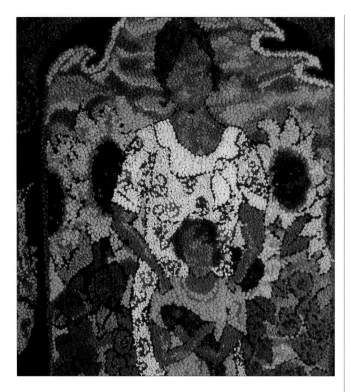

**Primitive Leaves,** 36" x 60", #6- and #8-cut wool on burlap. Designed and hooked by Deanne Fitzpatrick, Amherst, Nova Scotia, Canada, 2001. **Left:** close-up of **Girl With a Fish.**

On the floor, you need physical and visual flatness, and you can get away with a lot of distorted perspective. The neat thing about an unsophisticated perspective is that this type of rug can go on a wall or the floor. Usually a folk style, these mats make charming, decorative wall hangings.

The floor is more gracious to a flat or folk style. I'd almost say that the floor is "asking" for this. Over time, I've learned that the only rugs I really enjoy on the floor of my own home are the traditional style floor mats. I live in an 1840s farm house and these rugs suit my house. *Primitive Leaves*, at right, can be viewed from any direction. The center is simple, so it would be boring on a wall. It's ideal for my living room floor. Although the mat is large in proportion to the small room, the color is subtle, so it isn't focal point. If I lived in a big glass contemporary house the floors would be

screaming out for something completely different.

If you have a certain space planned for the rug, make sure that you size the work so there's space around all sides when it's placed on the floor. Otherwise, the rug will look as if it has been squeezed into place. Consider the colors already used in the room, but avoid obsessing on them. You want the rug to work in the room, rather than to look as if it was custom-made for it. I don't like a rug that's a perfect match. It should blend, that's all.

Some people prefer to hang their rugs on the wall, while others see rugs as only for the floor. In these days of eclectic design, any type of rug can go anywhere but, as always with decorating, in some places the rug will sing, in other places it will merely hum.

Thinking about how you want your rug to look is the first step in the practical part of the design process. I have a series of basic questions that should help you come up with a good idea of what you want to create. You can jot the answers down on a piece of paper, or just answer them in your head. I encourage my students to go through these questions every time they get ready to make a new rug.

- Is this rug being made for a particular place?
- Am I making this rug for fun? Will I decide the location after it's finished?
- How big should this rug be? A large mat—or one that looks large in proportion to the space it'll be in—is more likely to command more attention. In my house, for example, the rooms are 14' x 14'. Great big rugs don't look good on the walls.
- What shape should I make the rug?
- Do I want to add a border? Usually, a border that's more than 6" wide

makes a rug a dominant part of a room. Placing furniture on top of it will downplay this effect. A border with bold colors will draw attention.

- Will the piece be a strong statement—an attention-getter or a backdrop? You don't always need strong colors to make a rug a focal point. Placement, like above a fireplace or at the head of a table, will do the trick.
- What are my favorite colors? Do I want to use these, or create another color scheme?
- What look am I after? Would I prefer country, finely shaded, folk, primitive, serious, whimsical, story telling, or something else altogether?
- Will the intended location define the subject matter? For example, in a somber library you might not want a whimsical wall hanging of a woman dancing.

**Love and Forgiveness,** 32" x 80", #6- and #8- cut wool on burlap. Designed and hooked by Deanne Fitzpatrick, Amherst, Nova Scotia, Canada, 2002 , from the collection of Sharon Perry. The focal point of this rug is my father, yet he isn't dead-center in the rug. That position isn't always the best way to draw attention. Shifting him a bit, and adding the gravel path made the composition more interesting. Even though my father and the house are on the right side, the rug isn't off-balance. The car—especially its strong blue color—adds visual weight on the left, as do the slightly wider bits of grass. The house isn't overpowering because it's a soft yellow, and the roof blends with the hill behind it. Dark colors are often used in backgrounds because they don't pop. I broke the rules because my father is in a black jacket . . . yet he's obviously at the front of the rug. Placing yellow behind him made the difference. As you can see, composition isn't just about shapes. Using the right colors is just as important. Your goal is to get the viewer to rest on one spot—the focal point—for a few moments and then start looking at the other things in the rug.

We all know a great design when we see it, even if we can't say exactly what it is that makes the drawing work. What we're actually admiring is the composition. And, no matter how good a hooker is at showing movement and working with color, if the composition is off, the rug won't work.

For the most part, my approach to composition is intuitive. Many people approach rug design using their instincts. We draw a pattern, and then respond emotionally to the image. Then we fine-tune the drawing so that it "looks better." When we do this, we're actually organizing the elements of the rug design in a meaningful way. We're working with the balance of color, and shapes to come up with a pleasing finished rug.

I've been designing for more than 15 years, so I've spent a lot of time learning about composition. These days, it isn't something I think about a lot anymore, but it's part of every rug that I create. When I pull out a piece of burlap, I don't say, "I'm going to compose a rug." But I realize that composition is essential because I just know when the rug design isn't "right." This happens because, over the years I've trained myself to understand the elements of composition: balance, perspective, and focal point. One of the wonderful things about rug hooking is that as you are making the rug you can integrate some extra elements to enhance the composition. It's necesary to be careful when doing this because you can also throw the rug off-balance if you add too much.

If you followed my advice earlier in this book, to expose yourself to art (see page 18), then you've already started developing your awareness of good composition. You've been training your eyes to understand balance.

Developing your knowledge of balance also comes from "doing." You can place four or five templates on a backing and then, as you shift them around, rely on your intuition to decide when you have an attractive image. It'll be slow going at first, especially if you make one mat a year, rather than six or eight.

## Breaking Rules

Guidelines are helpful when you're starting out, so I'm offering some here. After you're familiar with them, take some chances. It's in breaking rules that we can make our greatest mistakes and, when we are on the money, our most original creations. By pushing the boundaries, you'll discover that people will respond more to your work.

▲ Avoid horizontal lines that go across the middle of a rug.

**My Life Before the NHL,** 6' x 2', #6- and #8-cut wool on burlap. Designed and hooked by Deanne Fitzpatrick, Amherst, Nova Scotia, Canada, 2000.

It'll divide your work so that the viewer sees two halves, rather than a whole composition.

▲ Use odd numbers for groups of items. If you're placing flowers in a design, for example, draw three, five, or seven. Even numbers of items, say two or four, aren't as interesting. The viewers eye will move around the rug more if there are odd numbers.

▲ Make sure that some element of the design demands your attention when you first look at it. This item is your focal point. Of all the elements of composition, the focal point is the most important.

## Fail to Win

You can learn as much from looking at a failed composition as from a successful one. If you don't like what you've drawn, try to figure out what went wrong. Everything that doesn't work brings you steps closer to a design that'll be great.

▲ Work with the colors and shapes, to make sure that the design has overall balance. Don't put all the visually heavy (larger, darker, brighter, more dominant) objects on one side of the rug.

▲ Establish perspective. A person standing at the front in a drawing is big, a house in the background is small, but if there's house beside the person, the house is much bigger.

Take a look at *My Life Before the NHL*, left. It has eight hockey players, but there are two groups: one of seven players and then there's another, single, player at left. Where the lake ends, there's a very strong horizontal line, which runs through the center of the picture. I can get away with this because the rug has an odd shape and the line is broken by the snowbanks, trees, and houses.

The simple design below is the first rug that I ever made. The classic simplicity of this stamped pattern drew me to it. It's perfectly balanced, with scrolls in each corner with leaves for a bit of interest.

We can learn a lot about balance from traditional and old mats. It's easy to create balance when you have a central image, with the same shape in all four corners. Some people break with tradition by drawing a unique shape in each corner. There's no way that the rug will have balance with such unusual shapes. Decorative and geometric mats need a sameness of shape in the elements.

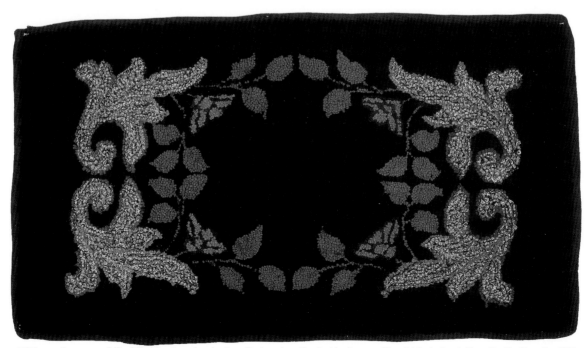

**Title unknown,** 34" x 20", #4-cut wool on burlap, Designed and hooked by Deanne Fitzpatrick, Amherst, Nova Scotia, Canada, 1990.

**In the Garden of Good,** 16" x 52", #6- and #8-cut wool on burlap. Designed and hooked by Deanne Fitzpatrick, Amherst, Nova Scotia, Canada, 2004. From the collection of Joan Beswick.

Lots of people are scared off by the word "perspective." Don't let the idea—and the way to achieve it—scare you off. Some folk rugs and primitive rugs throw perspective out the window, and that's a wonderful thing. In pictorials, however, the basic rules of perspective are important. You need to establish relationships between the elements in your design.

Like paintings and drawings, landscapes, and pictorial rugs are often described as having three parts: a foreground, middle distance, and far distance. The foreground is closest to you. An item placed in this part of a rug will be larger than the same item in the far distance, which is usually at the top of the rug.

To understand perspective, try looking at the world in a new way. Mentally "flatten" whatever you're viewing. A Polaroid camera can really help you get the hang of this. Take a quick picture of your backyard. Now look at the finished Polaroid while standing in the spot where you took the photo. You can even draw on the Polaroid (gently, with a fine-tip felt) to help you define the foreground, middle distance, and far distance.

Every afternoon I go for a walk. It's a great way for me to clear my head, enjoy the outdoors, and seek out inspiration. I spend a lot of time looking at things. As I walk down the road, I notice that a house next to me is huge and I'm small. I'm much larger than a house that's down the road and hills off in the distance. I get perspective by looking at the world

around me, noticing the proportions of buildings, cars, trees, and anything else that I come across.

So the main thing to remember about perspective in your rug design is that things that you want to look closer need to be drawn larger, and things that are farther away should be smaller.

For rug hooking designs, you don't need to master perspective. If you're really struggling with it, you might want to sign up for a drawing class at a local community center or school.

Try the quick activity, below, to help you understand perspective at its most basic.

## Making Your First Perspective Drawing

Creating perspective in a drawing doesn't have to be tough. Trust what you see. Here's a fun way to get started. Pretend that you're driving in your car. Try to picture the road. Have you ever noticed that it gets narrower as it goes into the distance?

1. Make a stickman at the bottom center of a piece of paper. This is going to be the foreground of your drawing.
2. Now imagine that your little man is standing on a road. Draw a straight line up the center of the page, to represent the yellow line that goes along the center of a road.
3. Now add your road, starting quite wide on either side of your stickman, and then angle the sides inward as you draw the two lines up the page.

## ▶ TIP  Mix and Match

Originality is about keeping your mind open to possibilities, about combining simple things that are all around you.

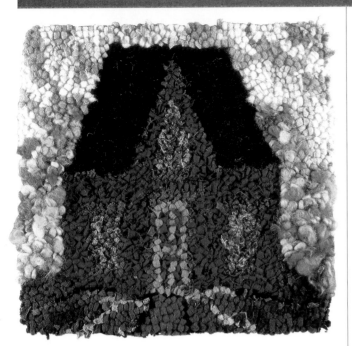

**Wine House with Roses,** 14" x 14", #5- and #8-cut wool on burlap.
Designed and hooked by Deanne Fitzpatrick, Amherst, Nova Scotia, Canada,
2004.

**Four Pitched Roofs,** 28"x 8", #6- and #8-cut wool on burlap. Designed
and hooked by Deanne Fitzpatrick, Amherst, Nova Scotia, Canada, 2004. From
the collection of Catherine Davis.

Even in the flattest folk rug, if there's more than one shape in the design, the hooker has arranged the elements—consciously or not—to be appealing. Composition is never thrown out the window. And a key part of composition is balance.

The photo above shows *Wine House with Roses* that I made with the house template that's included in this book. The little mat has static balance: a house in the center, a central sidewalk leading to a centered door, and the same amount of bushes and grass to the left and right of the house. This static balance lends a folk, or naive quality to the rug. It says everything is perfect when you know the reality of the world is never quite like that.

A pictorial rug, though, isn't the place to use balance that's so static. You want to create some mystery that'll com-

pel the viewer to react emotionally to your work. This is what I try to do with all of my rugs. Take a look at *Four Pitched Roofs*, above. Although still static, the balance is starting to look more interesting. There are four houses equally spaced along the rug. The shapes are all the same, so the interest comes from the colors. Each house is unique, so you have to wonder who lives in them. The added elements of design gets me thinking. The clouds in the sky aren't evenly distributed, and the house colors vary. By making the trim on one of the houses white, it appears to pop off the rug a bit more, almost moving into the foreground. The house beside it looks farther back because it's dark red.

So how do I create balance that isn't static? The answer is in the position of the shapes and colors of the rug design.

Still using the house as my example, I'll sketch it first. As soon as I do that, the house "asks" for more. When you're sketching, needs will arise and you'll respond to them. Like me, you'll add a tree here, a fence there. Creating balance is about setting shapes together in a fashion that works.

In *Shaped Coastal Houses*, below, I added another house. I don't like my focal points in the center of a mat, so the houses are off to one side. The lopsided positioning didn't look good without something on the right and I responded by adding water. The orange house was drawing too much attention so, in the very center of the foreground, I added some bushes. Everything in a picture doesn't need to be meaningful. Sometimes I include a rock, a bit of grass, a frond, or a wave in the water just because it adds balance.

**Shaped Coastal Houses,** 26" x 11", #6- and #8-cut wool on burlap.
Designed and hooked by Deanne Fitzpatrick, Amherst, Nova Scotia, Canada,
2004. From the collection of Marjorie Trenholm

What you're trying to do with good composition is achieve a sense of wholeness in the entire mat, not show every bit of every shape. Take another look at the house on page 30. It was the model for the house in *Wine House with Roses*, on page 38. My design doesn't include the large tree, the yellow insulation around the footing, or even the offset driveway at my neighbor's place. Those items didn't add to the balance I wanted for the mat.

You can omit or truncate anything that you want. You can cut a person off at the arm or show only a portion of a house, like I did with the orange house for *Shaped Coastal Houses*. Sometimes I leave out as much as I keep in. Things that are suggested, but not completely in the composition, can leave a viewer wondering. I think a rug works best when people continue thinking about what they see in my work.

Have you ever seen a photographer or filmmaker make a box with the thumb and forefinger of his hands, hold them in front of his face at arm's length, and then shift around? This isn't showing off. This is called framing a shot. The hands are creating a viewing area that will define the photograph. When shifting the improvised frame, the photographer or filmmaker is looking for the view that has the nicest composition.

You can do the same thing when you're sketching a subject or landscape for a rug design. Pick up several matte shapes at the local picture framing store, or cut your own horizontal, oval, and square shapes from cardboard. Hold up the matte and look through it, toward your subject. Notice how the edges of the matte frame the shape? Now shift the matte up, down, right, or left to re-crop your subject. What a difference this makes.

Watercolorists do this exercise all the time. I tell students that they need to think like a painter if they want to compose.

## ▶TIP  Believe in Yourself

Repeating statements may seem silly, but they work. As you go through your day, say things like "I am creative," "I can design," "I can draw," "I am an artist" and "I can create." Self-talk is a truly important part of your development as an artist. You may have a lot of doubt about your ability as an artist so you need to boot-up your courage and support your own efforts. Reassure yourself of your own possibilities.

## Finding a Good Frame

My friend, the painter Joy Snihur Laking, helps her students understand the importance of cropping and framing an image with a very simple exercise. You'll find it really helpful, too.

1. In two pages in your sketchbook, draw four different shapes: a square, a rectangle, a long narrow rectangle, and a fatter rectangle.
2. Within each of these shapes, sketch out the same idea in a way that's suitable for each "frame."
3. In the end, you'll have 4 different designs. Now you can make some decisions about what's working.

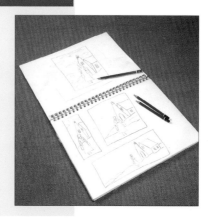

A rug needs a focal point. In other words, some element of the composition should stand out from the other parts of the design. The viewer's eyes will be drawn here first, and also rest longer on that spot. When some hookers decide a certain element will be a rug's focal point, they place it smack dab in the middle of the design. That's not what visual interest is about. Instead, the focal point is just the start of the viewer's experience.

It's true that a focal point will make a rug more interesting, but it shouldn't be the only point of interest in a rug. A good pictorial doesn't draw people to only one spot. Instead, it leads the viewer in and out of the design, drawing the eye to one place, and then to another. Mind you, the viewer is still looking at the entire work.

The focal point of *The Seven Sisters* is the woman second from the left, wearing the light pink scarf. She's larger and is wearing a lighter color, which makes her appear closer to you. Even though another sister at the far right is in a lighter coat, she doesn't command as much attention because she's smaller and tucked behind another woman in a dark-color coat. Your eye is pulled to the white coat next, then it shifts to the other women, the fronds in the foreground, then the dark background and, finally, the border. There's a lot to keep your eye moving.

There can be a tendency to add too many things to your rugs because you want it to be interesting. A rug does not necessarily become interesting because it has a lot in it. In fact this can be distracting and you'll end up with several items competing to be the focal point.

Decide on the important elements of your mat and make these interesting through the use of texture and color because these are the essentials of beautiful rugs. If you love to make rugs you'll have the chance to make many of them because you won't be able to stop yourself from hooking. Save ideas for future rugs rather than overcrowding a current one.

## ▶TIP Learning by Doing

Everything you hook doesn't have to be a work of art. You should be playful, have fun, and experiment with simple ideas. That's the pleasure in hooking. The most important thing is to just do it: make rugs. I've made rugs where the shape was a little off, or not quite right for the subject matter. In my time I have made plenty of mistakes in my rugs. It is not the mistakes that matter any more but what I have learned from hooking them.

**The Seven Sisters,** 4' x 5', #6- and #8-cut wool on burlap, Designed and hooked by Deanne Fitzpatrick, Amherst, Nova Scotia, Canada, 1995.

## ▶TIP Use What You Have

Rug hooking has a strong tradition of using what's on hand. As wool becomes increasingly less common, hookers will evolve to use what's available. I have noticed in the past few years that many people have tried hooking with polar fleece because it's readily available. Many people are sewing with it and have the scraps on hand. I think it's necessary to keep an open mind about materials if the craft is to grow. I still prefer to hook with wool, but if it wasn't available to me, I would hook with what I had.

A border is a great design element. It's the ideal spot to write a message or poem. It can draw attention to a rug's subject or it can further express the idea that's being shown in the design.

Years ago, borders were added to mats as a matter of habit and need. The borders were usually 2" or 4" wide, black, and sometimes featured scrollwork or leaves.

Traditional borders have strength They demand attention and create a frame around a rug. Sometimes they're as much an integral part of the rug as the subject matter they surround. When I put a traditional border on a contemporary design it acknowledges the traditions of rug hooking. In a way, a border can be a statement of respect for the past.

I still like to use the classic shapes and arrangements that were so common on early rugs: diamonds, leaves, roses, and vines. You can use a traditional element with a modern twist. For example, I'm partial to diamonds. I'll slip a bit of a diamond in here or there, as you can see in the detail of *Standing Before the Monument* below. I draw diamonds freehand. For a more geometric pattern you might want to create a template and get out your ruler to measure up the mat so that the diamonds are symmetrical.

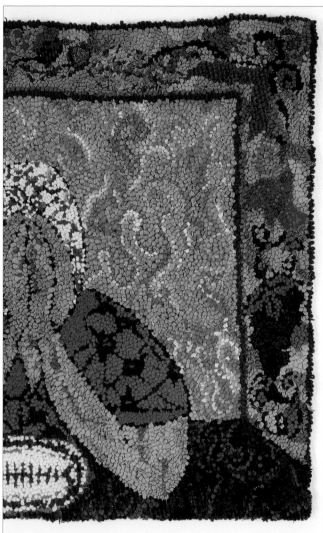

Close up of **Grace Mercy and Peace,** 32" x 36", #6- and #8-cut wool on burlap. Designed and hooked by Deanne Fitzpatrick, Amherst, Nova Scotia, Canada, 2000. This is an excellent example of a rug that emerges from a partial border. A border doesn't have to go all the way around a rug. I'm fond of hooking a border around only three sides, with the main subject emerging out of the fourth side. I like this because it breaks the rules and it makes the subject of the rug pop out. It gives a strong, clear focal point for the viewer to get interested in.

The border of *Grace Mercy and Peace* is mainly decorative, with a few symbols thrown in for interest. At bottom left, there's a raven, which reminds me of my mother. Irish ivy links the symbols so that it doesn't look like things are floating around the border. Also, the items in the border aren't mirrored around all three sides. Symmetrical placement isn't needed in this design. I'm more concerned about overall balance on the rug.

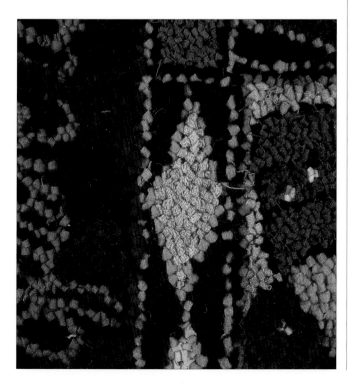

Whether you want to tip your hat to tradition, share an idea, work in a personal symbol, create some geometry, or add something that reflects your family heritage, a border is a great place to do so. For example, I placed Irish ivy on the border of *The Seven Sisters*, shown at right. With the last name Fitzpatrick, I'm sure you can guess why.

Flowers look good in borders, and they can do double-duty as symbols that reinforce a message. A lot of flowers have different meanings, and it's easy to find a book that explains them. When I have a free moment, I like to look through *The Grammar of Ornament: Illustrated by Various Styles of Ornament*. Originally published in 1856, it's an encyclopedia of decorative arts.

You can also find books and computer disks that have copyright-frcc borders. But I hope that you create your own borders, because inspiration is all around us. There are borders on clothing, plates, wallpaper. . . almost everywhere that you look. This means that you have an endless array of sources to inspire you.

Birds, branches, fish, flowers, fruit, grapes, leaves, seashells, vines . . . all of these things are good border elements. Often, I pull out one item that's in the rug design, and repeat that in the border. Let's say your rug shows a fishing village—the border could be filled with fish. A rug with a hockey theme could include a border of crossed hockey sticks. A border of pine trees could surround a rug that has an outdoor-theme. A border can even be a series of smaller borders—each with different shapes—that are stacked together.

Not all shapes have to be the same. A border needs continuity and flow, which does not necessarily mean there needs to be repetition.

I'll slip a little symbol or thought onto a border. In my work, you'll see a black bird—a crow. I may only use it once. You can repeat a symbol over and over, but it isn't necessary to do so to make your point. Just blend the lone symbol in with the rest of the border items. Slip it into the underside of a vine, balance it with a leaf, or position it in a corner.

I've seen people take a 6" wide border and stick in everything related to the rug's subject. The items look like they're floating. This collection might satisfy the hooker, but it isn't necessarily a good design. Symbols or pictures stuck here or there on a border don't always make sense. When you put all the elements in place, they should work together, have a sense of belonging to one another.

## Mocking Up a Border

A little pre-planning can ease any anxiety that you may feel about creating a border for a rug design. You can sketch some full-size examples on a piece of burlap, like I have done at right, or mock up a few designs on paper. A border is often a color puzzle. It needs continuity and pattern to the arrangement of color. A piece of paper is a good place to play with that.

1. Draw two lines near the top of a piece of paper. Now move down the paper a bit and draw two more lines, leaving room between them so that you can use the pair of lines as outer edges for a border design. Continue moving down the paper, drawing sets of lines with varying degrees of space between them.

2. At the top of the page, using colored pencils, draw a border design that uses the first set of lines.

3. Move to the next set of two lines, below. Draw another border design between these two lines.

4. Continue creating borders using the paired lines.

5. You can cut these out and lay them next to each other to see how they work on top of one another. Remember, borders are often layered on top of one another to make them more interesting.

The more that you look at other rugs and good art, and work on rug designs, the better you'll get at deciding what elements should be placed in a border, and how they'll be linked. And, equally important, you'll start breaking the rules. You might even decide that your rug doesn't need a border, like *Under the Covers of the Night*, at right. Without a border, a rug feels like it's going to extend beyond the edges. There's a promise that there's more beyond the picture. That's exactly what I intended. Putting a border on top of all this pattern would have confused the viewer, leaving her wondering what's going on.

Some rugs really need a border, usually the ones that give the message "it's all about what's right here."

How wide should a border be? This depends. What effect do you want? What does your intuition tell you? Do you want to break any rules?

The rule of thumb is that the border should be proportional to your mat. For example, if you added a 6" wide border to a 12" x 24" piece, all the viewer will see is the border. I'm partial to a 6" or 8" wide border for mats that are larger than 36" x 48". Mind you, this doesn't mean that I wouldn't use a 2" wide, solid block of color if that's what I felt the rug needed.

I'll even make one side of a border very wide, so that I can hook words into that section. The other three sides of the border could be very narrow.

Wherever you position words in a border, make sure

**Under the Covers of the Night,** 38" diameter, #6- and #8-cut wool on burlap. Designed and hooked by Deanne Fitzpatrick, Amherst, Nova Scotia, Canada, 2003.

that the area is 4" to 6" wide. Otherwise, the words will look squashed. Use your own handwriting so that yet another part of who you are goes into the mat. Hook in the words with a high contrast color, like wine words on a tan border, or red on black. Use slightly narrower strips (#6-cut works well) and hook tightly. This makes the words more readable. I never add words to a rug just for the sake of adding words. Always choose them carefully.

▶**TIP Add Flexibility with a Border**

You can make a pictorial look great on a floor by adding a border. It makes the image more emotionally and visually comfortable to look at the rug from all four sides, even if the rug design is oriented in one direction. Done well, a pictorial can look like a painting laid on the floor.

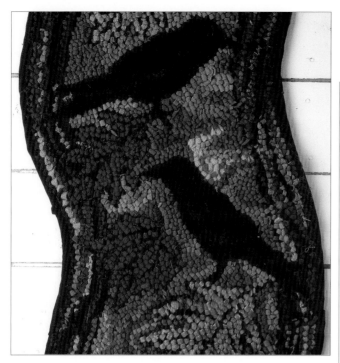

I like to let elements of a rug's interior break into the border. Sometime, a crow's tail or beak, a leaf, or a woman's foot will step over the line. This interrupts the flow, visually recessing the border. It makes the border just a little bit less important. You can see the effect in the detail of *Seven for a Secret Never Told*, above.

A border is generally less important to me than the rug's design. I treat it like the mat placed around a watercolor picture. All it does is frame the image. Sometimes I like it to have a bit of extra presence, and give the main body of the rug more punch at the same time. This is a delicate balance as the border could easily take over. Borders should be distinct from the main part of the rug. The easiest way to set this up is to place a line of color between the border and the main design. The line can be narrow and muted, for a subtle effect, or it can be a strong contrasting color, for a jarring separation. You can also use two or more lines of color for a stronger contrast and division.

Color has a huge impact on the border. The effect of the border color helps capture a moment, frames a design and pulls everything together.

Simply changing the border's color can totally change the look of the rug. When you want to give a simple frame, there's no better color than black or dark navy. It can also be useful to take the deepest shade used in the body of the rug and use that as a border. I find mixed tans a very useful background color in large, dramatic borders. It tones down the tempo, letting the subject of the rug come forward, while still allowing the border a bit of drama.

Using strong bright colors such as red, teal, or yellow will call attention to the border. It's essential that a decorative border such as vines or leaves stands out against the background if you want the features to be noticed. A brown vine on a wine border will be very subtle. It may work great but it won't stand out. Color planning for borders is just like color planning for the rest of the rug. You must be thoughtful in your approach to it. I have always found grays unsuitable unless they're very dark. They give the appearance of an absence of color. Of course, there are always a few exceptions. There are no hard and fast rules.

What's the purpose of a one-color border? There isn't one. It's just what feels right at that moment.

When I use a solid color for the border, I don't work with a single wool. There's a practical reason for this approach: I don't want to run out of strips of a particular color. So I'll mix together four or five wools that are all fairly close in color. The subtle variations add depth to the border. Wool in one color can make the border look flat and dull.

You can go in a totally different direction and just play with color, by making a hit-and-miss border. It's still a traditional treatment, and it's a lot of fun because all you're doing is hooking in strips of different colors. It isn't tough, although some say that it's hard to get the colors just right. The trick is to either pay careful attention to the order and balance of the color, or else totally ignore the colors. Merely pick a handful of every color that you used in your rug, toss these strips into a bag, and mix them up. When you're ready for a new strip, just grab one from the bag without looking at the color. The result is a very folk-inspired border.

A hit-and-miss border can be worked in squares, or horizontal or vertical stripes. One thing that you have to decide right away is the direction that you'll work: up or down, straight across or squiggly. Stick to your plan.

## Border Crossings

Over the years, I've noticed that some mistakes are rather common on borders. To help you avoid them, I'm listing them here.

- The border is too busy. It distracts the viewer, so less attention is paid to the rug's interior.
- The mat colors aren't repeated in the border.
- A small rug has a border that's so wide it's overwhelming.
- A border has been added to a mat that doesn't need one.
- The border is hooked in gray, or another color that drains life from a rug. This is the same as dressing in gray or black when it isn't the best color for you.
- Disconnected shapes are floating in the border.

**In the Churchyard,** 30" x 72", #6- and #8-cut wool on burlap. Designed and hooked by Deanne Fitzpatrick, Amherst, Nova Scotia, Canada, 2000. I decided on the shape of this rug after the women were centered in the image. It's interesting that the shape itself reminds people of a church steeple. I didn't set out to do this. I wanted it to be reminiscent of a church window, and I think it does show that as well. You can use the shape of a rug to reinforce the idea or message expressed in any rug, if you wish.

As I've mentioned before, much of my designing is done by instinct, which has been developed by continually looking at good composition. So there are times when I look at a sketch and know that I can reinforce the theme by shaping the edges of the rug that I'm going to make. You'll soon be doing the same thing. I usually just respond to a simple urge to shape the rug. I draw the shape and decide if it can stand on its own or if it needs a more regular, defined shape.

Shaping rugs is a new way of approaching an old art form. Traditionally, mats have been ovals, rectangles, and squares. Although I respect this history, I bring a modern attitude to my designs. For some of my pieces, I have been changing the shape of the backing by adding points or curves, or even trying out entirely new silhouettes. Mind you, I still make many, many rugs that are squares or rectangles.

Because I wanted to work with traditional materials, I started my rug hooking career with basic shapes. This was necessary because I was using feed bags for my backing. Once a feed bag is opened up, it's a large square. The shape of my mats was predetermined by this backing material. I branched out to rectangles, then a couple of long, skinny ones for runners. Next came ovals, which are still a traditional shape.

One day I noticed a wooden door topper welcome sign that had a curved upper edge. I looked at it and thought,

**Welcome,** 13" x 10", #6- and #8-cut wool on burlap. Designed and hooked by Deanne Fitzpatrick, Amherst, Nova Scotia, Canada, 2004.

"Wouldn't that make a great rug?" When I get an idea like that I run home and make it right away. The result was a hooked welcome sign with flowers. That's the first time I made a rug that was really defined by shape. The rug shown in the photo on page 45 isn't my first welcome mat, but I wanted you to see how simple your first shaped piece can be.

Eventually, I discovered rolls of 70" wide burlap. With so much length and width to play with, I now have all kinds of room to make shapes. This opened up a whole new realm for my designs. The wider a backing is, the more freedom you have to design and define your shape. My floor frame has rods that are 80" long. This also gives me extra room to create.

Soon, I started making wavy borders. The outside edges of the mat flow with the shape of the inner edge of the border. The edges are curved, like a woman's body. You can see this effect in *Leaves Falling and Crows*, on page 29, and also in *Fish School*, at right.

One of the things to consider when you're experimenting is how the shape and subject matter work together. In other words, the shape should enhance the subject matter. I'm not saying that some mats can't be shaped simply for a decorative effect. The welcome mat, for example, doesn't need a fancy upper edge. It's just for fun. But a shape can make a rug more dynamic.

Let's face it, square and rectangular mats are predictable. But a rug that has houses and hills . . . but no sky . . . will give the viewer a reason to pause. And what would have been a

**Fish School,** 20 x 34", #6- and #8-cut wool on burlap. Designed and hooked by Deanne Fitzpatrick, Amherst, Nova Scotia, Canada, 2004.

typical scene is now more interesting. If you decide to try this, I've found that it looks best if you cut off the entire sky at the horizon line. A sky cut off in midstream looks as if something is missing, or perhaps you got tired of hooking and decided to finish up. Of course, everything can be done well, but some things are harder to do.

▶**TIP** Dreams of Success

When I make shaped rugs of villages I often refer to them as dreamscapes. They're small, quiet little places that only exist in my mind. These shaped villages, with their softly rolling hills, are one of the types of rugs that are most recognizable as my style. If you decide to create a shaped village rug, be sure to consider the following suggestions:

- Don't make a shape that's full of jagged edges. These will be impossible to bind without cutting so close to the hooking that you risk cutting the rug itself.
- Use interesting dark wools in the back hills. Try different plaids, tweeds, and fancy wool yarns that lead the viewer back.
- Don't be afraid to put a bit of brightly colored wools in the back hills to represent a few houses or flowers off in the distance.
- To approximate flowers in the foreground, hook in some natural sheep's wool in bright colors and highlight with a bit of green sheep's wool.
- Tweeds for the roof can approximate shingles. Avoid solid colors that flatten out the surface. Include a chimney, a third color for the window trim, a ladder on the roof, heck, even a man on the ladder. The interest in the rug can be in the details.
- Don't hook a solid line of color all around the dreamscape. It'll cut it off, overemphasizing the shape and taking the viewer away from the subject matter.

**Little Coral House,** 7" x 7", #6- and #8-cut wool on burlap. Designed and hooked by Deanne Fitzpatrick, Amherst, Nova Scotia, Canada, 2004.

You might want to work on small projects, to get your feet wet. Hot mats are a good starting point because they don't demand a lot of your time. The usual way to make a mat would be to trace the house template inside a square, and then hook a square mat. Rather than squaring off a mat, why not end it around the roofline, as shown in *Little Coral House*, above?

I often make hot mats that are in the shape of a house, slightly rounding the peak. Gentle curves and soft edges are easier to work with when you're binding. Sharp edges are hard to sew without cutting too close to the hooking. I found that you can make uniquely shaped smaller items such as fridge magnets and tree ornaments by spreading white craft glue on the back side of the hooking and over the edges. After drying overnight, you can cut right around the hooking without fear of fraying.

Drawing the lines for a new shape isn't tough. What's most important is making sure that you can finish the rug's edges. If they're gently curved, then all you have to do is gather and tuck the edge of the binding as you sew it in place.

Shaped edges are a bit challenging to bind. Ask yourself if you have the patience and skills to bind a point or jagged edge. You might end up with a bit of burlap showing. I take these bits, refold them, and then hand sew them once again so they can't be seen from the front.

I usually leave about 2" of burlap beyond the outermost loops of the border. I hand-sew the binding near this last row of loops. Next, I fold all of the burlap and binding to the underside of the rug, and then loosely hand sew it all in place. You can see this effect on the rug that I'm holding at right. For floor rugs, I used cotton or nylon thread and black

cotton twill tape. Nylon is strong, but cotton is less likely to eventually cut the burlap backing.

Honestly, though, I like rugs directly against a wall, without any kind of binding. I just fold the excess burlap to the back, tuck under the raw edge, and loosely hand sew the burlap in place. Without binding, it's easier to finish the shaped edges. In fact, for very jagged edges (90° angles, for example) it's easiest to fold and glue the excess burlap to the rug's back using white craft glue. I wouldn't use this approach for anything but a small wall hanging since the finishing affects wearability. I don't worry too much about the quality of the finishing on my rugs. As long as the front looks good, I'm happy.

▶ **TIP** Listen to Your Rug

In 1999, I received a letter from Judith Gibbins, who lives in the United States and has hooked for many years. She wrote:

"Some of my students never seem to put themselves into the rug. I often wondered if it was because the patterns they chose didn't warrant it. I like to hook at night when all is quiet, and I can concentrate, think, and pray. And, in the light of day, I am sometimes amazed at what I've done. I'm not really taking credit for it, but simply knowing there was a moment that was beyond my consciousness."

Now this woman has style. She has given herself the freedom to get into her work, letting it develop rather than trying to dictate and control it. You need to get lost in your hooking, and become responsive to it. When you add one color or texture, the rug will start to call out to another in response to it.

## CHAPTER FIVE

# Secrets of Style

We all started rug hooking with basic, simple designs that were probably heavily influenced by the work of other people. There's nothing wrong with this but you shouldn't do it forever.

Over time, you've probably started finding your own style; maybe holding your hook the way it felt comfortable, rather than the way your mentor showed you. Or perhaps you noticed a preference for textured wools? If you get together to hook with friends regularly, people in your group might even be able to identify your mats without looking for your signature. This means that you have already started creating your own style. For example, the photo on this page doesn't show a rug, yet it clearly shows my style—nature, asymmetry, interesting textures, and subjects and symbols in my work.

Style is what makes your work distinct from that of other hookers. In this chapter, I'm going to explain how to discover and nurture your distinct style. Then I'm going to talk about color, movement, and texture, so you can experiment with elements of style that I feel are important.

**A Small Child's Dream of Home,** 24" x 12", #6- and #8-cut wool on burlap. Designed and hooked by Deanne Fitzpatrick, Amherst, Nova Scotia, Canada, 1991. The rug depicts the house that I grew up in, with the church nearby. My dad had a workshop in a little shed across the street. This is one of my earliest mats, made as a study for what turned out to be the cover of my book *Hook Me A Story.* This is a good example of how design skills develop over time, with practice. I love this rug for its charm and simplicity. For me it is a marker of where I started, and it's a symbol of my childhood.

My work is freer now than it was a decade ago. It's influenced more by what I see through my own eyes, rather than the work of other artists. It took me a while to trust myself. I've become more interested in the way oil painters makes their strokes—the way they approximate a distant hill in paint—than I am in the overall image or the inspiration for it. There is alot that can be learned from oil paintings because the thickness of that medium has similarities we can copy when hooking our wool.

uthenticity is another word for style. Style is about speaking in your own voice and choosing methods and techniques that express your values and beliefs. It's about seeking out personal inspiration. Your style can be in your subject matter, the way you pull your loops, the materials you work with . . . just about anything that's part of designing and hooking a rug.

When I started hooking, for example, I wanted to use the same materials and techniques as the East Coast Canadian hookers who established traditions long before I was born. This became part—but not all of—my style. Over time, I started shaping the outer edges of rugs, introducing natural lamb's wool and metallic threads, and developing more abstract compositions. I let myself move in another direction. It's the dream of every artist to develop a sense of style without stagnating. Style isn't about doing one thing.

How can you go about nurturing your own style? You can start with a conscious decision . . . or not. Without any conscious effort, I find myself adding personal symbols to my mats. There'd be seven women, or seven crows, for example. I'm the youngest of seven sisters so it makes sense that this theme would emerge again and again. You might find yourself

## Believing In Yourself

It's important to trust yourself and enjoy what you're doing. Don't think about every loop that you pull. This can become a chore. Rugs hooked with this type of intensity end up looking more like a series of loops rather than an overall rug. Get lost in the hooking, so that your mind can wander and you can become meditative. The beauty of hooking is getting lost in the process. It's wonderful to look up from the frame and see that an hour has passed and you've a great deal to show for it, even though you barely knew time had gone by.

To help you give yourself over to the motion of hooking, you might want to try this exercise.

1. Set yourself up in front of your frame, with hook, and wool in hand.
2. Close your eyes. Now start hooking. Don't worry about making mistakes. The idea is to sense how your hands are working together. Think about the motions you're making and how one hand is working with the other.
3. Turn on some classical music and hook some more, this time with your eyes open.
4. Compare how your hooking changed when you altered your environment a bit.

repeating a theme or subject without realizing what's happening. These items could become part of your style and, once you're aware of this, you might decide to work that theme.

The best thing that you can do to nuture your style is practice. But, honestly, you can't find your style by hooking a rug every three years. Creating style is about building a body of work. This could mean making a rug every year for 12 years, or six rugs over three years.

Note that I'm suggesting hooking several rugs over several years. You don't have to race to create a whole lot of work. Don't expect your style to evolve that quickly. It takes patience, practice, time, and a whole lot of attention to your inner voice. Style can be subtle as it develops. It's not often that you'll have a dramatic change. Instead, there will be small, simple things that are different, or consistent, from one rug to the next. You won't notice these until you've been hooking for about three years. That's when you'll have enough pieces that you can look at them all together and see the themes and changes.

Materials can also be part of your style. Grenfell Mission rugs from northern Newfoundland and Labrador, for example, are defined by silk stockings that were hooked straight across the backing. Cheticamp hookers use fine yarn. And Acadian women still hook with T-shirts and jerseys. Some students come to workshops with T-shirts, and I say, "Use what you've got, and what makes you feel good." Who am I to impose my style on them?

Style can be defined by the way that you hook. My content varies yet the way that I hook is always identifiable. I hook rather loosely and pull my loops high. They often have a twist in them. The way I make my loops is comfortable. Hooking in your natural style is necessary if you're going to repeat the motion again and again . . . and again.

At my workshops, once in awhile I'll see a person beating herself up because she isn't hooking "right." Somehow she has gotten a message the loops have to sit a certain way

▶**TIP** **Explore Your Inner World**

Sometimes, you need to start with self exploration to create your own style. Here are some questions that I encourage hookers to ask themselves:

● What are my basic values?
● What are the stories I want to tell?
● What am I trying to express in my rugs?
● What's unique about my life?

## Visualizing to Boost Style

Most people would find it easier to develop their own style if they would let their bodies relax. Anxiety and worry aren't good for creativity.

When you feel yourself getting tense, a relaxation exercise can help you get your imagination and creativity going again. This activity will also improve your ability to visualize rugs during the planning stage. For this exercise, ask another rug hooker to read the following steps to you while you imagine a world that could be translated into a seascape rug. As you see the scene, try to think about the whole idea, rather than bits of it.

1. Close your eyes and breathe deeply.
2. Imagine being in a kitchen. Get up and walk out the back door. Standing in the yard, look down toward the water.
3. See a boat coming into the wharf.

and be a certain height. I always feel somewhat sad for them. The way that a person hooks is as individual as her handwriting. It might be fun to experiment a little, like you did when you copied your mother's signature when you were a teenager. But, as happened with your signature, you'll always gravitate back to your natural habits.

I'm not saying that you shouldn't try new things. Experimenting helps a style evolve. My message is that you own your own hands. Don't let anyone tell you how to use them, especially if that way does not suit you. Respect—your natural style—it's the least you can do for yourself. Appreciate what your hands can do, and work with them, rather than against them.

Some people just do floral rugs or they just do geometrics. For many years my rugs were defined by the idea that they had a story. I even wrote a book called *Hook Me a Story*. I'll probably always create pictorials (also known as story rugs) but I now do other kinds of mats, too. I'm quite happy making a mat that's simply decorative. The hooking then becomes an exercise in color. Yet, in all of these situations, my style is still maintained because it isn't only defined by content.

I read about a couple who only hooked pigs. I sometimes hear people say, "She's the one who hooks cats," or "She's the one who hooks a yellow rose in the corner of every mat." This is subject matter, and it may be an element of style, but style isn't just about a specific subject. It's about the character of the work. It's all of the elements put together. These give people an indication of who the hooker is as a human being, and how the hooker is responding to the world around her.

**Coming Down from the Mountain,** 44" x 51"; #6- and #8-cut wool, eyelash yarn, roving, sheep's wool, silk ribbon on burlap. Designed and hooked by Deanne Fitzpatrick, Amherst, Nova Scotia, Canada, 2004. For texture to work, some loops have to be pulled high, so that they come up off the rug and have strong definition. Yet there still has to be a flat quality to other areas. Originally, I hooked a woman into this rug. She had her arms up and open, expressing awe for nature. Every time I looked at the completed rug, I felt that that there was too much in it. I took out the woman, and found I preferred it that way. Now that's what I call an absence of want.

The woman looked too flat. It was almost impossible to give her any dimension. This is one of those problems that people have to deal with when they work textures into landscapes. You can over-texualize the rug, adding too much everywhere. It's important in field rugs such as this to use lots of texture, but place it strategically. It might take a long time to figure out how to solve a problem, but it's important to have these kinds of challenges.

Texture adds dimension and depth to hooked rugs. Along with color, it's what creates the wonder and joy that's part of all fabric arts. Texture is an essential element of expression. It takes a rug from a flat surface to an interesting textile with sculptural qualities. It makes a person want to reach out and touch a rug, to feel the fibers. It's an element that draws the viewer into the rug, so that she's more than an outside observer.

Texture is a way to lead the viewer's eye around the rug, giving it good composition. It also adds perspective because one part of the rug will stand out, while other parts recede. Somehow, adding texture to a rug makes it seem more real, more picturesque. I like it for landscapes, in the clouds, rocks, and sea. I also use it for animals and hair on people.

Many rug hookers are comfortable with plaids and tweeds. These do give a bit of a textural effect. But it's the warmth and softness of heavily textured materials, such as carded wool, hand-spun and slubbed yarn, lamb's wool, and cloth from bouclé jackets, mohair throws, and paisley shawls that add extra dimension to rugs. Natural wool right off the goat, llama, or sheep can be washed and used as-is or dyed. Some people even hook hair that they've combed off their dogs.

No material should be dismissed outright. Our job as artists and designers is to find a place where texture is needed, and then seek out a suitable material. I was astounded once by a comment made during a visit to a group of Acadian women in Shediac, New Brunswick. When I asked about a mystery material in one of the rugs, the group coordinator responded with a laugh, "Oh, that hooker uses chip bags sometimes." I was enchanted, not because she chose chip bags, but because she was willing to try anything. Her mind was wide open. The scrunchy looking metallic of the chip bag was an interesting highlight. It caught my attention.

It took me a awhile to try heavily textured materials in my mats And that there might be some rug hookers who disagree with my use of yarn and other non-traditional fibers. It is perfectly fine to decide not to use certain materials in your rug. I will probably never hook chip bags, but I respect that someone else might want to experiment and I encourage you in this direction.

When I was first making rugs, I avoided using yarn. It reminded me of the latch hook kits. Most of the wool yarn I came across was spun very neatly and dyed in plain colors. It didn't have much to offer. Friends like Heidi Wulfraat soon changed my opinion. I fell in love with the colors and textures in her yarn shop, London Wul Farm in New Brunswick. (see "Sources" on page 72).

On my last visit to her place, I found some yarn spun from the hair of her rabbits. Tucked on another shelf was a mohair blend yarn and an eyelash yarn (long strands hanging from a central core). I thought both of these yarns would look nice as the base of a woodland area. A gold-and-orange silk ribbon caught my eye. I "saw" leaves falling. There was a blue-and-orange silk yarn that was perfect for where the turned leaves meet the sky. With the rovings (very loose wool) I had at home, I knew that I could make a forest come alive. A color plan took shape. I'd been on a long, long hike just the week before. This memory, and those special yarns, were enough to get me going. *Coming Down from the Mountain*, on the previous page and at right was the result. Who can look at these beautiful hand spun, or hand dyed wools and not be inspired to create?

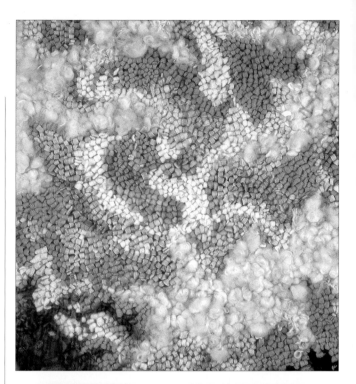

Natural sheep's wool makes great clouds, as you can see at right. It's also wonderful for big, fluffy waves in an ocean. When you dye sheep's wool it can be used for the sky or the sea. It can also be dyed in yellows, pinks, and oranges and be used to give the impression of flowers. I like the way it pops out to give a bushy effect. Using this type of texture makes a sky feel larger, and gives it a billowing feeling. I like to hook three different textures in large patches for this effect.

Students often ask me how to hook natural sheep's wool because it's so loose and fluffy. I like to take a bit of the material and pull it gently until I've stretched out a 5" or 6" length. (See the photo at right). Now I hook the length the same way that I would a piece of cloth. (See the photo bottom right). I do tend to pull the loops higher. I also let the loops stand out from the rest of the rug. You have to hold it gently, almost keeping it together as you hook it.

Natural lamb's wool, both dyed and undyed, is great for hair. Haul the loops up slightly higher than the loops of cloth. You want the hair to stand off the head, for a more life-like effect. I like to leave a strand or two loose, on the surface of the rug, to show movement in the hair. To me, it makes the hair look like it's blowing in the wind.

When you hook natural sheep's wool in thin, spindly lines, the sky looks as if it's divided so try to hook it in larger billowing patches. In a seascape, you can hook rows of unspun wool under the waves to give them extra presence and strength.

Very thin wools such as serges and men's suiting hook in as a thready texture that's great for showing movement in a sea. Be on the lookout for heavier woven fabrics, such as plaid coats or boiled wool jackets. I've always used mohair blankets, coats, and scarves. They dye easily and make wonderful texture in fields and skies. Sweaters, long woolen underwear and even old woolen socks will add a fluffy dimension to your work. When I shop in secondhand stores for wool I always check the women's sweater bin for baby blue angora, or orange silk jersey, and the green merino wool to highlight the fields in your next pictorial.

Some highly textured wool cloths or sweaters may need to be hand cut into strips. I've found that they're either too bulky or too limp to feed through a cutter. I have an excellent cutter with interchangeable blades, but I still can't get a cut that's wide enough for sweaters. You can often cut highly textured wool or sweaters quite wide, sometimes up to $3/4$", as they are soft and pull up easily through burlap.

To make really wide cuts, I don't bother measuring carefully and then cutting through a single layer at a time. That sort of precision is lost to the eye when the texture is hooked in. Instead, I fold cut the textured fabric into flat pieces. As shown in the photo at right, I cut through about four layers after folding the yardage several times. I just eyeball the width. Uneven strips are part of the charm of primitives.

For landscapes, you can use almost anything in nearly any shade. Golds, rusts, and other autumn shades will show the earth as somewhat parched, or as it is in the fall in northern climates. Bright yellows, purples and reds will stand out as flowers. Greens will look like dimension in the land or bushes. I like to use multi-colored wool that's spun thickly in some areas and thinly in others (called slubbed) because the varied quality changes the look of the land. Right now I'm working on a spring rug full of browns and mauves. I was surprised to see how much mauve there was in a spring brook.

Recently, I was charmed by a small skein of Italian silk ribbon that was dyed brown, gold, and rust. The silk wasn't a pleasure to work with. I sometimes ended up grabbing my thumb or finger with my hook. Expect this to happen when you're working with thin material. I would never hook silk ribbon in a large area, but worked into the details that you can use to make a rug sing, or even do a jig (a dance where I come from).

**Coming Down from the Mountain,** 18" x 50", #6- and #8-cut on burlap. Designed and hooked by Deanne Fitzpatrick, Amherst, Nova Scotia, Canada, 2004.

### Beautiful Clouds

An angora sweater is truly wonderful because of the way that it curls when you cut it wide. Pulled through a backing, it gives your mat a bubbly texture. This is nice for showing a bit of light or movement in a field, the side of a hill, or the sea. It can be great for clouds. I like to use it alongside natural sheep's wool because it gives a little more height than cut cloth, but is not quite as high as the sheep's wool. It acts as a lead into the drama of the sheep's wool.

If you're using a fine yarn or very thin fiber, it's a good idea to strand several bits together when you hook, so that the fiber will be more pronounced. I have strung three, four, even five strands together. If you want fine texture for a background, or if you don't want the thin fiber to jump off the mat, try hooking it as a single strand.

The photo at right, shows me pulling through three strands of silk at the same time. This isn't difficult because you're constantly pinching the strands together as you hold them underneath the backing. When you want some height with silk or fine yarn, you really have to make an effort to pull up the strand. Place the loops tighter together than usual. You'll end up rubbing your forefinger and thumb against one another and against the hook. Over a long period of time this can be painful. I wouldn't recommend using these fine textures for a background. They're best used in small amounts, for detail.

Fragile fibers and wools also need special handling. I still work with them because I like the effect of old, loosely woven blankets hooked into a rug. But I cut the wool wide (#8-cut or higher), and hook carefully. As you can see in the photo at right I hold the strip loosely in the hand underneath the burlap, and then use my fingers, as well as my hook, to gently push and lift the strip through the backing.

Fine bits of metallic cloth, silk, and linen will shift your rug away from ordinary and bring it into the realm of art. When the subject calls for it, I like to add bits of metallic fabrics or threads into key points in the rug, like the fish in *Girl with a Fish*, at right. Fish are a wonderful place for gray wools. Grays often look dull unattended but when we shimmer them up they come right to life. I stranded a metallic thread together with a wool as I worked around the eye and down the side of the body. Remember that adding metallics will draw the eye to that area of the rug.

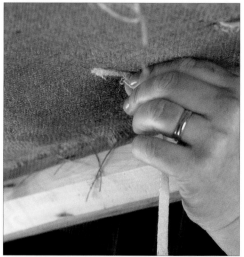

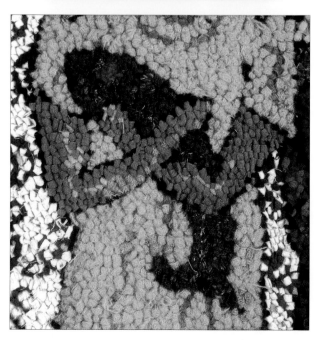

▶**TIP**  **Find Time for Style Exploration**

Artistic style evolves because a rug hooker is open to experimentation, new techniques, and self-exploration. But the key component is practice. Good art is the result of labor. You have to commit your time to the process of developing your own style. In fact, when you start, all you need to do is find the time to explore. Learn what you like to use for materials, how you like to use them, how you like to hold a hook. Once you put all of these elements together and start designing and hooking, your style will arrive naturally.

I like to give people who come to the studio a visual treat. I hang yarn and roving around the studio, tuck hooks here and there, and stack pieces of wool in baskets. In this photo you're looking at the second floor of my studio. When I first came to this house the upper floor was gray, dark, and uninsulated. You could see the roof boards above your head. It has come a long way from those dreary gray barn boards and now is host to colorful mounds of wools, and baskets of roving.

The ceiling is low, and the room was dark until I installed a skylight. This was important to me because I like to choose my colors in natural daylight, and I figured that customers might feel the same way. Often, our busy schedules require that we hook in our free time, at night. If this is your situation, still choose your colors in the daytime. Set them aside, knowing that you're going to hook them later. Choosing color in the natural light allows you to see how your choices are interacting with each other.

Color can be an important part of your style. The hues and tones that you put in a rug can often speak quite clearly about your feelings. Over time, you'll probably notice that you tend toward certain colors, or that you like to work with a certain range of hues. My rugs, for example, are full of many colors. Even if I'm working with a somber palette of brown, taupe, and black, I can still have up to 200 variations of those colors. I like to think that nothing is ever one color, because color is always affected by light. As long as light is falling on an object, then there are several shades in it.

Your style will resonate in the colors you choose. The way you feel about the world, and your view of things may very well show up in the tempo of the colors you choose if you truly immerse yourself in the rug that you're making.

If there's one thing that I want you to take away from this book, it's the message that you should exercise and trust your intuition. Respond to it and it will become stronger. Make your own judgment about color instead of relying on someone to lay it out for you . . . or merely picking a scheme off a color wheel.

I don't really work up a color plan for a rug. I have an overview in my head, and then I introduce new colors as I'm working. An artistic approach to color is always a process. It's not a plan. Think of architectural drawings for a house. You follow the plan as you build, but you sometimes move a door a little to the right or left, add a closet, or even put in another room. This is the approach I encourage you to use in your mats. Get an overview of the color scheme, and then add a little here and there. Take away what doesn't work for you, and continue to make adjustments to get it just right.

Theory says that it's a good idea to place color so that it moves the viewer's eye around the mat. Say, placing a touch of red throughout so that there's continuity. I do a bit of this, but it's instinctive. If you're struggling with color, though, look up one of the many books for artists. Sometimes knowledge can reassure intuition. Remember that you're just reading guidelines and keep these ideas in the back of your mind. Knowing the rules will help you break them successfully. It may be handy to have a book on the shelf, but use it for reassurance, rather than to chastise yourself.

What colors do you really like? How do those colors make you feel? What colors give you energy? Look around your house for color schemes that you have created. Look in your closet to see what colors you pick for the clothes you wear. What color schemes stand out? Most of us know what we like. Use what you like in your rugs.

You can't force yourself to work in colors that you don't respond to. I have watched people working with a color palette that's not of their choosing: they have no feelings for the rug. They might even avoid finishing it. It may be one of the reasons you can't quite get back to a project that's on your to-do list. Try approaching the project from a different color perspective.

The emotional place where you are in your life will affect the way that you deal with color and the way that you respond to it. If you're in a really dark period, you could find that a rug full of vibrant colors might overwhelm you. I'm not talking about your mood from day-to-day. These are just quick feelings. The emotions that you have in a period of your life will come out in your rugs, if you trust your intuition.

There's nothing wrong with working in darker colors, and you can still use colors freely. Sometimes what you can do with three or five colors, all in the same range, amazes me. Simple plans of four to six colors can work beautifully in a primitive style mat. It doesn't have to be complex to be

## Dye for Inspiration

My color palettes are ever-changing. They can be influenced by things I have no control over, such as the next bag of woolens that I find at the secondhand store. Although I use as-is wool, I still dye.

I like to work without recipes, experiment with color. I then put the dyed wool into my cupboard. I don't generally dye wool for a particular project. Over the last few summers I hired an art student, Joanna, to help in the studio and dye wool for me. I have a small, but beautiful, old barn that's been renovated to hold my wool. In it, we set up a small kitchen so that Joanna can dye large quantities of wools at a time. On hot summer days, we pour boiling hot water into plastic ice cream buckets, add the dye, put in the wool, put a lid on the buckets, and then let everything sit in the hot sun for the day. When we get the color we want, we pour in vinegar (ten parts water to one part vinegar) letting it set until the water is clear. Joanna spreads the wool on drying racks or a clothesline. Joanna can have as many as 12 ice cream buckets set up as dye vats in the hot summer sun. It's a beautiful thing to see the wool hanging over the barn doors. It's a feast of color for the eyes.

This sun-dying process also works well for natural sheep's wool, which we spread on the grass to dry. I love to drive up and find the lawn and drying racks filled with fabulous blues, golds, and greens that are waiting to be turned into landscapes.

good. In fact, introducing too many colors can sometimes ruin a rug, making it muddy and confusing.

When I did the show "One for Sorrow, Two for Joy," my mats were expressing the transition of a community. There was a lot of loss and the colors in that show were somber. This doesn't mean that I was "dark" in the mid-90s when I made the rugs for the show. It's just that what I felt about the community was loneliness and want. The darker palette expressed that mood to the viewer. People who saw that show often say to me now that my colors are so different. They see a difference that I initially failed to recognize because I was immersed in the project rather than objective about it.

In a later show, my mats were full of bright colors. The theme was women and, since I was raised in a boisterous household with six sisters, the body of my work expressed a thankfulness and a warmth.

There's contentment and joy in my life, so my underlying emotions when I hooked works for both shows was the same. The impact on the work was subtle, but you can see it throughout. The subject matter really affected my color choices. I didn't start a piece by thinking, "Oh, this is a happy topic, so I want lots of yellow in it." Instead, I immersed myself in the subject, so that my emotions and intuition would lead me to a suitable palette.

If you're just learning to express yourself through color palettes, and learning to develop your own color style, don't get discouraged. There are very specific things that you can do to work out colors for any rug that you're working on.

● **Visualize the completed mat.** Spread similar colors, or bits of the same color, across the pattern you've drawn on your backing, as shown on page 57. This will help you visualize a sense of balance and continuity in the rug. Try to work with colors that have similar tones (the amount of gray that's in the color). If one or two colors are completely different, they may create a jarring effect that you don't want.

- **Choose a basic palette.** You probably already have an image in your head, or an idea where you're going. If you're working on a fall woodland scene, for example, you're probably planning on lots of brown, gold, and red. A winter seascape, on the other hand, will call for blue and white.

- **Seek inspiration.** Pick colors from a favorite painting. I'm inspired by impressionist painters as well as folk painters like the mid-20th century artist William Kurelek from western Canada. You can see how nicely the wools, which are in colors I pulled from this painting by Alfred Whitehead at right, work together.

- **Get an overview.** It's a good idea to keep some wool cut and ready to use. But when you want to make decision about a color for your mat, look at a nice, big piece of wool. It's easier to size up color looking at a piece of whole cloth, rather than staring at a strip of wool.

- **Build a stash.** You can never have too much wool in your cupboard. Collect, organize, and manage your wool so that it's accessible. If you can afford it, get the bit of alpaca, but make sure you can find it when you need it. The perfect piece of wool in the bottom of a cardboard box in the basement will be no good to you.

- **Pull out your wools.** If your materials are piled together in a plastic bin you can't see what you have to work with. I have a big cupboard (some would call it a wardrobe). When I start working on a new piece, I pull out all of the wool that has hues and tones that are in my basic palette. Then I stack everything on the shelves in my cupboard. When I make a turn on my frame, I'll decide that it's time to add a new color, swing open the doors on my cupboard, and make a choice.

- **Keep color front and center.** I work on a Cheticamp table frame. So I place bundles of wool in front of me, on the frame when I'm working. Having only two or three strips of color in front of me, using them up, and then pulling out three more isn't the way to work. This approach would suspend my ability to use color freely.

- **Examine color in nature.** I often look outdoors for ideas on combining colors. Once, while snow-shoeing, I was taken aback when I took a close look at a birch tree. I had always thought that birch-bark was white and gray, but it has a multitude of colors.

Start looking carefully at landscapes. Outside your kitchen window notice how the light of day affects the color of the sky. It'll change from blue, to gray, to pale yellow . . . and even orange, purple, and red. Water isn't always blue and grass isn't always green.

**Practice with paint chips.** Collect a few paint chips that have suggestions about colors that go well together. These are your foundation. Now choose some other paint chips with colors that you think would go nice with the foundation. Place them on top of the first three and see what happens.

**Revise your plan.** For me choosing and planning colors is most often a gradual process. When I choose one, it'll influence my next color. For example, the type of red that I use in one area will affect the gold that I pick out for another area.

**Practice visualization.** Close your eyes and try to imagine the ways colors will look together. Take the rug you're currently working on and try to picture it with a series of different color backgrounds.

**Copy a plaid.** A plaid fabric is already an attractive, unified color plan. If you find a plaid that you really like, pick out the individual colors in it. Now match these to your wools.

**Take a break.** If you're stuck on a particular area, leave it be. Go back to it later with fresh eyes, rather than staying focused on the area, hooking it, and then having to rehook it again and again.

**Study what you like.** Flip through a magazine or go through your collection of postcards and pull out photos and illustrations that appeal to you. By studying these, you can begin to understand the colors that the photographer or artist used to create mood. It might help if you try to pick out colors and match them to wool in your stash. You don't have to hook the wool. Observing should do the trick.

**Look at printed fabrics and textiles.** Some designer has already created a color plan for these fabrics. Use the color-matching sidebar that you find on the edge of fabric as a guide.

**Learn to dye wools.** There's nothing so inspirational as the colors you make yourself. I often want to hook them before they're dry enough to use. When I see the colors I think, "Oh that will be great for rocks, or a summer field, or her dress." The dyed wools get me thinking.

▶**TIP Mix and Match**

I often use traditional floral, leaf, and scroll borders, even if the rug designs are more contemporary and pictorial. I like to mix the old-fashioned and new elements. Traditional borders show respect for the history of rug hooking.

## Hooking in Your Head

My Cheticamp floor frame is very wide, but narrow. So I can only see one section of my rug at a time. Yet I usually pick colors as I go. I'm often asked, "How do you know what color you need, and the overall shape that you're hooking?"

It's all about the picture that's in my head. Visualization is an important part of the way that I design. You can learn to visualize your completed rug, which is very freeing for the design process.

Here's a group activity that can develop your visualization skills. Have someone read the steps while the rest of you sit comfortably. Pay close attention to the details, because these can be worked into your designs, and it's the details that'll make your rug richer.

1. Close your eyes.

2. Imagine all of the rooms in the house where you grew up.

3. Walk next door to the neighbor's house. Go up the steps and on to the porch. Remember what was there. Is there a hammock or a rocking chair? What color is the front door?

4. Walk into the kitchen. See the floor, the table, the pictures on the wall. How does the kitchen smell? Pay close attention to the details. Walk through your neighbors house.

5. Now imagine some new scenes:
   • A pregnant woman in a yellow checked dress, sitting at a table with a red gingham tablecloth. She's eating ice cream.
   • A willow tree by a river. A boat is sailing by.
   • Two dogs at the side of a dirt road, fighting.
   • A man asleep on a couch. He's snoring and about to fall off the edge of the piece of furniture.
   • A cool wind blowing over a field of wheat. It's September.
   • Smoke billowing from a pipe.

Close-up of **Getting the Rural Mail.** The fun part of making this rug was pulling up the heavily textured trees along the left side. I added a few small bushes in the right background to balance the texture. I find that pulling up tufts of dycd, natural (untwisted) sheep's wool in the foreground of a landscape will approximate bushes that show a lot of movement.

A student told me that one of the greatest things she learned at my workshop is that she should say, "bush, bush, bush . . ." when she's pulling up loops for a bush. Essentially, what she meant was that she should get lost in what she's doing. She should think about the area of the rug that she's hooking, and to hook it like it is what it is. She was going to think about the subject, and hooking in the direction that would best suit it. For example, why hook a slanted roof any other way but on a slant?

Put some energy and movement into your hooking, so that energy and movement will show up in your rugs.

You can bring a rug to life by giving the content some movement. This could be a matter of making branches look like they're moving, adding folds to the skirt of a dancing figure, or drawing a hockey player with her arms in the air. Expressing any movement can be done by the way you draw the subject, the colors, and materials that you use, and the way that you hook.

When I draw people I try to make the lines soft, almost letting my hand shake a little as I draw the lines. I also hook outlines loosely, rather than straight and stiff. When was the last time that you saw a straight hem? Probably in a store, looking at a dress or skirt on a hanger. As people move, their clothing shifts around them. Even standing still, clothing can be a bit off-kilter because we tend to lean or slouch. So I like to soften clothing, and imply a bit of movement by making the tail of a woman's dress hang a little lower. This makes it look like she's leaning to one side. You can see this effect in the bit of the mat shown at right, which is called *Women in the Evening Light.*

Be careful how you shape a droopy hem, or tail. If it's too large, or the garment color is overpowering, then the skirt "tail" is all that the viewer will see. The mystery of other elements

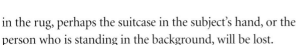

in the rug, perhaps the suitcase in the subject's hand, or the person who is standing in the background, will be lost.

In the photo above left, to enhance and define a fold in clothing, I sometimes start the shape by hooking a black line. This is the same kind that you'd use for outlining a shape in primitive hooking. The black line is never straight. It's used only to emphasize the fold.

Once the fold is defined, I'll apply color to both sides of the black line, as shown in the photo above right. In this example, I'll apply two shades of gold: a mid-range and a slightly darker color. This makes the fold look as if light is falling on the clothing without getting into a complicated shading process.

Movement is often shown in primitive hooked rugs through the use of simple shading. Unlike some other methods of hooking, shading for primitive hooking does not require that you use many different values of a similar color. I like to mix several, perhaps two or three, that are very close, depending on the size of the area that needs to be covered. Sometimes a deeper tweed can be used to accent the lines or the folds.

When hooking a sky, it's tempting to pull a different color out of the bag every time you need a new strip. Don't do it. This approach will lead to a striped effect, kind of like a random hit-and-miss. Instead, aim to hook bodies of color that vary in size. Fill in areas that are at least 3" to 5" by 4" in amoeba shapes, never squares, or rectangles. Think of making organic shapes. In other words, use one color to fill a small, randomly shaped area, then go on to the next area. The photo at left shows how the color areas look as they're being worked up.

The first time that you try this, you'll probably think it looks a bit odd. Don't give up until you've hooked at least a square foot. Now stand back and take a look. It's hard to assess the effect when you're too close.

I like to hook this type of sky with an upward motion,

using long, thick strokes of color to approximate the movement sky's movement. In contrast, the sky on a sunny day would be worked differently. You could make a few clouds by hooking large, shaped areas of color. I might work with wools in three pale blues, each one only slightly different from the others.

There's no right or wrong way to hook the sky for day or night. There are many right ways, and some ways that don't work as well as others. For example, if you hook the sky straight across it will look striped. I have seen many skies hooked with darkest values used at the bottom, and colors varying until the lightest values are hooked straight across at the top. It's clear in these rugs that the hooker has been following the rules rather than expressing her idea of a sky.

One of my favorite places to show movement is in a sky. A large rug of a night sky can sometimes require 10 to 15 shades of various blacks, blues, navies, purples . . . and even greens. All of these colors were hooked into the sky of *Hockey Night in Nova Scotia*. This is one of my favorite night sky rugs. I believe the colors in the bouclé yarn, which I used to enhance the sky, end up illuminating it.

People often comment on the sense of movement among the players. There's plenty because the children's arms and legs are positioned in many poses. My family breathes hockey in the winter months. I don't skate, but I've spent so much time watching the kids on the rink out back at my home, and sitting in the stands at the local arena, that their movements have sunk into me. It's this intense exposure to the skaters that made it possible for me to draw them in the midst of their game.

Backgrounds and borders don't have to be dull, flat, uninteresting elements of a rug. You can show movement by hooking in swirls and curlicues to get a sense of dimension and movement.

Every summer I make several mats that include swimmers in them. The detail of the rug, at right, has a sky that was hooked in many mid-blues. You can see the entire rug, called *The Swimmer* on page 66. One of the blues is a tweed that has a bit of red in it, as I thought that would be striking against the red bathing suit.

This rug also includes blues for the water. I used dark tone, though, to contrast with the sky. A couple of lines of black emphasize the curves of the woman's body and imply the motion of the water. Sometimes, I like to use very similar colors to emphasize movement, rather than resorting to shading with color.

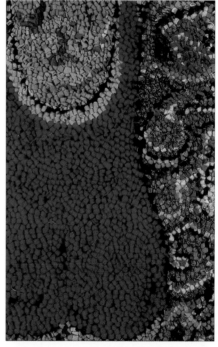

## Bagging a Landscape

Have you ever taken a moment to really look at a field? Just once, try counting the colors. It's surprising how many browns, golds, greens, rusts, tans, and wines you'll come up with. I have a simple method to help you blend colors when hook a landscape.

1. As you cut your wool into strips, sort it into three piles: light greens, medium greens, and dark greens.
2. Put each of the sorted piles into three separate bags. Bag one for the light colors, bag two for the mediums, and bag three for the darks.
3. Take a handful from the first bag and put it in the second bag.
4. Take a handful from the second bag and put in the third bag.
5. Use the lighter colors (in bag one) to hook the foreground.

6. Use the medium greens (bag two) for the middle of the landscape and some of the lighter colors in the first part of the middle ground.
7. Use the darker colors (bag three) for the back hills, remembering to accent the front part of the background with the handful of mid-colors you put in it.
8. Finally, add other elements throughout the landscape: bits of texture, gray or tan for rocks, in the midst of the landscape.
9. Now explore some fun options. What would happen if you put a bit of purple in the back hills, or a bit of royal blue? You'll just have to try it to find out.

## CHAPTER SIX

# The Gallery

Many of my favorite rugs and all of my current projects are on display in my studio. This is a rather quaint affair that's attached to my house.

My family and I still call it "out back" because we couldn't live in the space when we bought the house. It was a barn for the original cabbage and turnip farm. There was even a "Barn Dance" sign over the door and, on the second floor, bunk beds for farm-hands. Somehow I became attached to the old barn. Even on the advice of my favorite contractor (who also is married to my sister), I couldn't tear it off and start again.

The studio came about when part of the floor fell in and we decided to renovate it so that it could be a warm usuable part of the house.

Now people come to visit the studio almost every day—for a swatch of wool or to buy a piece of art. Everyone likes to see the rugs hanging.

I figured that people who can't make the trip to Canada's East Coast might like to see what I've been working on. So, in this section, I'm going to show you 16 of my pieces and explain a bit about their origins and their creation.

*Getting the Rural Mail* is about expressing an idea, but it's also a powerful story rug. It tells about the people in an East Coast village coming together, and how collecting mail in a rural area can be an event.

The cottages at Amherst Shore, near where I live, have always been small clapboard or shingle-clad houses. They're just big enough for a family, and small enough that you want to go outside and play. Sadly, they're disappearing. This rug, which shows a plain farmhouse against the scant remaining cottages, reminds us that we're just passing through, and a small place will do just fine.

I like to keep the ocean and the sky quite different colors so the horizon line is obvious. Several closely related blues are used to give the sky a soft effect. The ocean is silk yarn and darker blues from old blankets that I dyed. The headstones are several different whites. The largest headstone is hooked from a sweater that had lumps in the fabric. I like the way that the lumps approximate stone and give the headstone extra impact.

**Getting the Rural Mail,** 48" x 64", #6-, #8-, and hand-cut wool, natural lamb's wool and silk yarn on burlap. Designed and hooked by Deanne Fitzpatrick, Amherst, Nova Scotia, Canada, 2004. From the collection of Lynn Bishop.

**In the Churchyard,** 30" x 72"; #6-, #8-, and hand-cut wool on burlap. Designed and hooked by Deanne Fitzpatrick, Amherst, Nova Scotia, Canada, 2000. From the collection of Joy Laking.

The balance in this rug is simple: there are two women positioned to either side of the center. Yet there are variations. The back of each woman is a slightly different distance from the closest border. I like to eyeball these things. If you fret too much about having everything perfect, your finished rug will look as if all of the content was carefully measured.

The wave along the bottom of this border emphasizes the coastal roots of the women who are whispering outside the church. The subject matter could be seen as friendship, or as gossip in the shadow of religion. I like to leave a little mystery in my rugs. It's not what I put into them that matters as much as what the viewer takes away. The narrow border of vines was made by pulling random colors out of the mat.

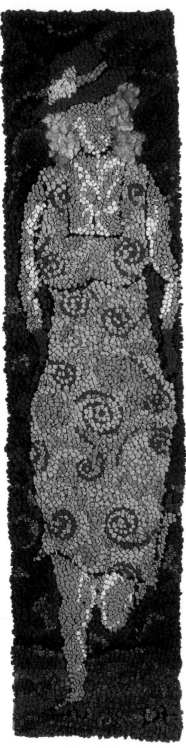

**Hat and Glove Kind of Woman,**
14" x 50"; #6-, #8-, and hand-cut wool on
burlap. Designed and hooked by Deanne
Fitzpatrick, Amherst, Nova Scotia, Canada,
2004. From the collection of Anne and
Kevin Major.

**The Beauty of an Idea,** 4' x 5'; #6-, #8-, and hand-cut wool on burlap.
Designed and hooked by Deanne Fitzpatrick, Amherst, Nova Scotia, Canada, 2004.
From the collection of Fiona Black and Andrew Wilson.

This rug started with a desire to hook a field of flowers and express my belief that an idea is a beautiful thing. The design emerged when I noticed that some painters create fields of color that angles straight across their canvases.

I struggled with the short verse for nearly a day before I settled on its final form: "Wild flowers crowd my mind, color my thoughts, engaging too much space, not enough space to thoughtfully draw each one, petal by petal, for the love of a single flower, but as a whole for the beauty of an idea."

As I hooked the words at the bottom of the rug, I almost tore out the multicolored effect many times. I felt I was making a mistake. I'm glad I took the risk. I went for a walk when my doubts were strongest. A crow flew out of a ditch, startling me. Then it dawned on me that this bird would be great in a bottom corner of the rug. It's a focal point in the stately bushes, and is a great tool for showing distance.

In this day and age, what kind of women wears a hat and gloves? I like to think she's a free spirit. She has drama and energy. She also started life as a dancing girl. My son saw what I was creating, and said, "She needs a hat and gloves, Mom, for your hook-in." At the time, I was readying the studio for my annual Hat and Glove Hook-In, where visitors come for a day of hooking and are encouraged to dress in the suggested attire.

I enjoy changing gears a little as I hook a rug, adding a new dimension as ideas come up. This is part of the creative process. Rigidity will only lead to stiff-looking rugs.

The color combination for this rug—deep royal blue against a lemon-lime green, is one that always works. Throw in a bit of rusty red, and you're shaking, baby. It's a combination of color that gives a "what's happening here" feeling.

**Irish Angels Watching Over Bay Girls,** 54" x 120"; #6-, #8-, and hand-cut wool on burlap. Designed and hooked by Deanne Fitzpatrick, Amherst, Nova Scotia, Canada, 1999. From the collection of Joan Beswick.

My family grew up around "The Bay" rather than in Newfoundland and Labrador's only city. Women who weren't from the city were known as Bay Girls. This rug was inspired by an early photograph of my sisters, which was taken before I was born. They were standing outside our house in their little bandanas, looking cold and poor. I thought that there must be Irish Angels (my grandmothers and great grandmothers) looking over them. This rug is about the bonds in life and beyond the grave. I'm making a statement about how we're cared for, and linked to people we barely know.

The filament-like wool for the angels' wings came from a wool sweater that I gently pulled up. The flaming red hair is slightly higher than the rest of the rug so the angels stand out. The coarse gold wool of the tallest girl's coat was an old bouclé coat. I mixed in a little solid gold to show a few fabric folds. I often use a tweed for bandanas because it approximates a calico effect. I hooked several tans and camel hair skirts to get the effect of light falling on the faces.

I like to show women realistically. Women are beautiful because they're beautiful, not because they're thin. This particular idea of showing just the dress emerged because of the way women are sometimes viewed in society for their bodies more than their minds. It's a parody on the standards that society and women set for themselves.

It's always a challenge to choose an outline color for black clothing. You really need a highlight, rather than an outline. In this case, I chose a gunmetal blue tweed to enhance the breasts and define the fabric folds. There's some navy mixed in with the black, so that it looks like light is falling in different places on the dress. I trimmed it with white for a startling effect.

The white in the pearl choker is slightly different because it was hooked with a white, loopy bouclé yarn. I used a multi-color, single-ply cotton/rayon yarn to hook a pattern of diamonds all over the dramatic red background.

**Little Black Dress,** 20" x 36"; #6-, #8-, and hand-cut wool and cotton/rayon yarn on burlap. Designed and hooked by Deanne Fitzpatrick, Amherst, Nova Scotia, Canada, 2004.

**The Swimmer,** 22" x 38", #6-, #8-, and hand-cut wool on burlap. Designed and hooked by Deanne Fitzpatrick, Amherst, Nova Scotia, Canada, 2002. From the collection of Jennifer Melville King.

**Coming Down From The Mountain,** 44" x 51", #6-, #8-, and hand-cut wool on primitive linen. Designed and hooked by Deanne Fitzpatrick, Amherst, Nova Scotia, Canada, 2004. From the collection of Bob Gerheart and Susan Huxley.

Most of my summers are spent in a cottage on a rust-colored, sandy beach. For years, when I looked out to the sea, I saw only one or two shades of deep blue in the calm water. One day I looked out and finally saw what had always been there: a riot of color in the swimmers. This discovery led to a whole new set of ideas for rugs. It's important to observe the world around you, even the things that you think are commonplace. What's ordinary one year may be inspirational the next.

Tufts of sheep's wool emerge from underneath the swimmer's bathing cap to approximate a few loose curls of hair.

This is both a story rug and a field rug. It began with a hike I took to Economy Falls, Nova Scotia. It was a six-hour hike with four friends. We followed the path winding through the splendid colors of autumn. On the way out we took what we believed to be a shorter route. It wasn't, but we didn't know that at the time. About halfway through the return trip, two of us started laughing and couldn't stop. How much longer? We had no idea. There was no chance that we'd be home to meet our children getting off the school bus, and our cell phones couldn't get a signal. We did make it to a phone in time to call someone to greet the bus.

It's a day like this, and the splendor of nature, that I wanted to capture in the rug. Just after I started it, I visited a yarn store and came home with silk and mohair, to enhance the leaves. They are pulled freely to higher levels so that the color stands out from the fields. I left the sky large so that I could convey the feeling of the vastness of nature.

**Blueberry Fields in November,** 6' x 4', #6-, #8-, and hand-cut wool on burlap. Designed and hooked by Deanne Fitzpatrick, Amherst, Nova Scotia, Canada, 2004. From the collection of Robert G. Christie.

This rug started as a floor mat, so there aren't any textured yarns and wools in it that would catch on toes. I overdyed a bright rust with black to dull down the original wool that's used as the main body of the rug. I wanted to emphasize the color that blueberry fields turn when they are touched by frost. When the rug was complete, I did put it on the floor. But every once in awhile it would be hung for a photo or a show.

I discovered that I liked it better when viewed straight on, rather than from above. I put the branches in the corner to add a little perspective. The binding was created for the floor, yet it serves as a nice frame when the rug is on the wall.

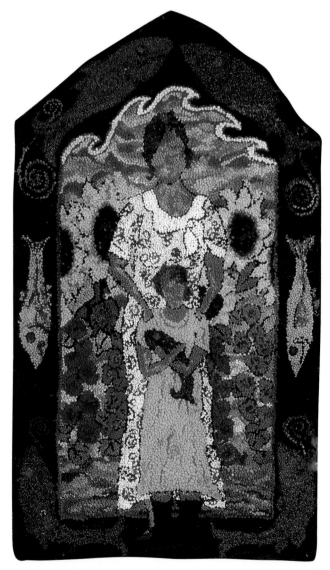

**Girl with a Fish,** 40" x 70", #6 and #8-cut wool and metallic thread on burlap. Designed and hooked by Deanne Fitzpatrick, Amherst, Nova Scotia, Canada, 2004. From the collection of Anne McCaffrey.

This rug was an interesting project. I wanted to convey the love between a grandchild and grandparent. The image is based on a story that was written by Anne McCaffrey, called "A Fish Named George." It's about summers that the author spent with her grandmother. I often will be inspired to create a rug based on the written word. As the words flow through my brain, pictures are created in my mind. This is the gift that every good writer gives to a reader.

The fish in this rug were fun to detail. I used bits of multicolored yarn in the eyes, fins and tails. I love to hook fish eyes because I get to use funny pink wools that seem to have no other use.

**Grace Mercy and Peace,** 36" x 32", #6- and #8-cut wool on burlap. Designed and hooked by Deanne Fitzpatrick, Amherst, Nova Scotia, Canada, 2000.

I love the rich, vivid color combination that's set against the mystery of the subject matter in *Grace Mercy and Peace*. This rug hangs over my kitchen table, which people can see when they enter the studio. It interests me that so many people define the content differently. I like the ambiguity of the heavy-set woman holding her head in her hands . . . or is she praying? As I hooked this rug, many emotions were going through my head. This rug reminds me of my mother and inspired a poem.

**Women in the Evening Light,** 56" x 65", #6-, #8-, and hand-cut wool on burlap. Designed and hooked by Deanne Fitzpatrick, Amherst, Nova Scotia, Canada, 2004. From the collection of Pugsley's Pharmacy, Ltd.

## Cod's Heads

*Some bit of memory*
*swimming in a pot of Cod's Head Stew,*
*of a woman who convinced me as a child of eight*
*that they were fit to eat by letting me eat just the potato*
*until I lifted the skin of the fish*
*and found the sweetness of the cheek.*

*To the sound of sucking*
*on the hollows of the cod's head,*
*as a child of nine I cleaned my plate,*
*leaving clean white needles of bone.*

This large rug is really about women being lovely and beautiful at all stages of their lives. It's also an expression of friendship. I'm reminded of my mother and her friends standing together. It seems that their dresses always peeked below their coats and that they covered their hair with bandanas for protection from the wind.

In this rug, you can see how the coats are hooked. To approximate the folds in the fabric, I used two or three colors that are nearly the same. Tufted bits of wool give the grass a bog-like, spongy appearance. The wools in the evening sky show a lot of activity because I wanted this area to also work as a background.

A photo in a city newspaper, taken by Ted Pritchard, inspired *Standing Before the Monument.* In the photo, a group of survivors are standing before a monument to the Halifax Explosion. The women had all been babies when the city was destroyed by a huge explosion of a munitions ship in the harbor. I'm not often inspired by things like this, but I couldn't get the image out of my mind. I loved the way the women looked, and how they seemed to be reflecting on their lives.

After I made the rug I realized that I hadn't hooked the people in the newspaper picture. My subjects turned out to be the older women who made up my life. I saw the woman I buy flowers from at the market, my own mother, a neighbor, and a woman I know from church. It was as if the slant of their shoulders, and the tilt of their heads had sunk into my unconscious and came out in the mat. They're clearly recognizable to me and to others in my community.

**Standing Before the Monument,** 8' x 6', #6-, #8-, and hand-cut wool and hand-spun yarns on Scottish burlap. Designed and hooked by Deanne Fitzpatrick, Amherst, Nova Scotia, Canada, 2002. From the collection of Arif Samad.

**Hockey Night in Nova Scotia,** 34" x 32", #6- and #8-cut wool on burlap. Designed and hooked by Deanne Fitzpatrick, Amherst, Nova Scotia, Canada, 2003. From the collection of Adele Mansour.

This rug was a gift for my daughter. She loves to play hockey . . . as does my son . . . as does my husband. I'm surrounded by ice each winter because my husband floods the yard to create an outdoor rink. Each weekend from September to April we're at the local hockey rink. I can't skate, but I've come to enjoy this bit of my life. There's no telling where your children will lead you.

I pulled up many different whites to make the snow and ice life-like and give it a shimmer. When I look at the snow, it sparkles a little, which is the effect I wanted.

**Three Nuns**, 32" x 14", #6- and #8-cut wool on burlap. Designed and hooked by Deanne Fitzpatrick, Amherst, Nova Scotia, Canada,1997. From the collection of Joan Beswick.

I went to a school that was run by nuns. Many of them still wore habits, although their skirts were shorter than the traditional ones. These nuns introduced me to the arts. I'm so grateful for an education that taught me that there's more to learning than math, reading and writing.

*Three Nuns* is an example of a dreamscape, where repetition and pattern are mixed with reality. I love to play with the reality of my past and present, and give images from these times a surreal quality. This could mean I'll draw fishermen dancing on the wharf ( it never happens), or nuns lining up along the coast. These types of rugs are playful and fun.

This is one of my early shaped rugs. It has an organic quality. At this point, I was beginning to leave behind the rectangles and starting towards the shaped door toppers.

This was one of the first rugs that I made that featured people and a night sky. You can see that it's so much simpler than ones that I made in later years. In the beginning, I used only one or two navies or navy tweeds for skies. Since then, I've learned that dark skies can be a riot of color.

I've come to accept that in this medium I'm only approximating a night sky. This means that I can play with color. An artist once told me, "Draw it the way you see it, not exactly the way it is. If you want it exactly the way it is you can take a picture." Making art is about creating a vision. You're showing your view of the world.

With this rug, I learned also what I can do with people as a group and as individuals. I loved using so many colors in the clothing. It was a starting place so it still gives me with a good feeling.

**New Year's Eve in St John's Harbour,** 62" x 30", #6- and #8-cut wool on burlap. Designed and hooked by Deanne Fitzpatrick, Amherst, Nova Scotia, Canada, 1993. From the collection of Joan Beswick.

# Sources

The following is a list of sources for the many materials and techniques discussed in this book. Keep in mind that this is only a partial list of the many companies that sell these products. Most of these companies, and many more, advertise in Rug Hooking magazine. These companies can get you started with all the supplies needed to make hand-hooked rugs. The rest is up to you. Enjoy!

**Rug Hooking Magazine**
1300 Market Street, Suite 202
Lemoyne, PA 17043-1420
(800) 233-9055
*www.rughookingonline.com*
*rughook@paonline.com*
The indispensable source of rug hooking information and advertisers. Annual subscription for just $27.95.

**Beehive Hooking**
Laura Schulze
3611 River Oaks Road
Tigler, TX 75707
(903) 566-4522
*www.beehivehooking.com*
All supplies for hooking rugs, kits, and finished rugs as well as a journal on the website.

**Bruce Grinding & Machining**
PO Box 539
Bridgewater, NS B4V 2X6, Canada
(902) 543-7762
Bolivar cutting machines.

**By the Door Hooked Rugs**
Deanne Fitzpatrick
RR 5
19 Pumping Street Road
Amherst, NS, B4H 3Y3, Canada
*www.hookingrugs.com*
(800) 328-7756
Complete line of supplies, kits, and patterns.

**Castle in the Clouds**
7108 Panavista Lane
Chattanooga, TN 37421
(423) 892-1858
*castlerug@comcast.net*
*www.geocities.com/castlerug*
Fleecewood Farm Patterns, including *Pumpkin Boy*.

**Cox Enterprises**
10 Dube Road
Verona Island, ME 04416
(207) 469-6402
How-to videos and books on hooking and braiding for beginners and advanced crafters.

**Cross Creek Farm Rug Studio and School**
Burton, Ohio
Beth Croup
13440 Taylor Wells Road
Chardon, OH 44024
(440) 635-0209
Workshops and Katherine Porter patterns, By appointment only.

**Dorr Mill Store**
PO Box 88
Guild, NH 03754
(800) 846-3677
*dorrmillstore@sugar-river.net*
*www.dorrmillstore.com*
Quality wools, color palettes, patterns, kits, and much more.

**Emma Lou's Hooked Rugs**
Emma Lou Lais
8643 Hiawatha Road
Kansas City, MO 64114
(816) 444-1777
Primitive rug patterns.

**Fredericksburg Rugs**
15001 Walden Road, Suite 100
Montgomery, TX 77356
(800) 331-5213
*www.fredericksburgrugs.com*
*fredrugs@consolidated.net*
Complete rug hooking supplies, hand-dyed wool, wool by the yard, patterns.

**Green Mountain Hooked Rugs**
Stephanie Ashworth Krauss
146 Main Street
Montpelier, VT 05602
(802) 223-1333
*www.GreenMountainHookedRugs.com*
Patterns, supplies, and the annual Green Mountain Rug School.

**Halcyon Yarn**
12 School Street
Bath, ME 04530
(800) 341-0282
*www.halcyonyarn.com*
*service@halcyonyarn.com*
High-quality rug yarn for finishing hooked rugs.

**Harry M. Fraser Company**
433 Duggins Road
Stoneville, NC 27048
(336) 573-9830
*fraserrugs@aol.com*
*www.fraserrugs.com*
Cloth-slitting machines, hooking, and braiding supplies.

**Hartman's Hooks**
Cindy Hartman
PO Box 938
Hudson, OH 44236
(330) 653-9730
*hhooks@mac.com*
Hartman Hooks.

**Heirloom Rugs**
124 Tallwood Drive
Vernon, CT 06066
(860) 870-8905
*www.heirloomrugs.com*
*heirloomrugs@aol.com*
Supplier of Zeiser, Skatet and Hookraft Designs

**Heritage Rug™ Hooking**
13845 Magnolia Avenue
Chino, CA 91710
(909) 591-6351
*www.mcgtextiles.com*
Complete rug hooking and finishing supplies.

**Hook Nook**
Margaret Siano
1 Morgan Road
Flemington, NJ 08822
(908) 806-8083
*www.hook-nook.com*
Lib Callaway rug patterns, hooking supplies, and instructions.

**Jane Olson Rug Studio**
PO Box 351
Hawthorne, CA 90250
(310) 643-5902
(310) 643-7367 (fax)
*www.janeolsonrugstudio.com*
The total rug hooking and braiding supplier for 33 years.

**London Wul Fiber Arts**
Heidi Wulfraat
1937 Melanson Road
Lakeburn, NB, E1H 2C6, Canada
(506) 382-6990
*www.thewoolworks.com*
Specialty yarns and fibers.

**Morton Frames**
311 Park Street
Winfield, KS 67156
(620) 221-1299
*Country@kcisp.net*
Rug hooking frames.

**Patsy B**
Patsy Becker
PO Box 1050
S. Orleans, MA 02662
(508) 240-0346
*patsyb@c4.net*
Over 250 primitive patterns.

**PRO Chemical & Dye**
PO Box 14
Somerset, MA 02726
(800) 228-9393
Fax: (508) 676-3908
*www.prochemical.com*
Dyeing supplies.

**Pris Buttler Rug Designs**
PO Box 591
Oakwood ,GA 30566-0010
(770) 718-0090
*prisrugs@charter.net*
Pris Buttler patterns, including *Lamb's Tongues and Sunflowers*.

**Rigby Cutters**
PO Box 158
249 Portland Road
Bridgeton, ME 04009
(207) 647-5679
Cloth stripping machines.

**Ruckman Mill Farm**
Susan Feller
PO Box 409
Augusta, WV 26704
(908) 832-9565
*www.ruckmanmillfarm.com*
Susan Feller's rug designs.

**Spruce Top Rug Hooking Studio**
255 West Main St.
Mahone Bay, NS, B0J 2E0, Canada
(888) RUG-HOOK
*www.sprucetoprughookingstudio.com*

**The Wool Studio**
706 Brownsville Road
Sinking Spring, PA 19608
(610) 678-5448
*www.thewoolstudio.com*
*rebecca@thewoolstudio.com*
Quality woolens, specializing in textures for the primitive rug hooker. Send $5 for swatches.

**W. Cushing & Company**
PO Box 351
Kennebunkport, ME 04046
(800) 626-7847
*www.wcushing.com*
*rughooks@wcushing.com*
Dyeing supplies, hooks, patterns, kits, and much more.

**Woolley Fox, LLC**
Barbara Carroll
132 Woolley Fox Lane
Ligonier, PA 15658
(724) 238-3004
*www.woolleyfox.com*
Primitive patterns, custom kits, Gingher scissors, and other supplies.

**Woolrich Woolen Mill**
Catalog Orders
Two Mill Street
Woolrich, PA 17779
(570) 769-6464
(Ask for Mill Sales, ext. 327)
*rughooking@woolrich.com*
Factory direct rug hooking wool.

**Yankee Peddler**
Marie Azzaro
267 Route 81
Killingworth, CT 06419
(860) 663-0526
Cutters, hand-dyed wool, hooks, and patterns, including *Museum Bed Rug* and *Bed Rug Fantasy*.

## Acknowledgements

*I have had wonderful help creating this book. I would like to thank Ginny Stimmel and the gang at Rug Hooking Magazine who are creatively pushing the boundaries of the craft, Susan Huxley for great organization, and Robert Gerheart for the fine photography. Thanks to Brenda Clarke, Louitta Sears, Joanna Close, and Cathy Carter for all their hard work in the studio and still remaining patient and kind to me. And, of course, thanks to Robert Mansour, my good husband.*

### ABOUT THE PUBLISHER

*Rug Hooking* magazine, the publisher of *The Secrets of Planning and Designing Hand-Hooked Rugs*, welcomes you to the rug hooking community. Since 1989 *Rug Hooking* has served thousands of rug hookers around the world with its instructional, illustrated articles on dyeing, designing, color planning, hooking techniques, and more. Each issue of the magazine contains color photographs of beautiful rugs old and new, profiles of teachers, designers, and fellow rug hookers, and announcements of workshops, exhibits, and gatherings.

   *Rug Hooking* has responded to its readers' demand for more inspiration and information by establishing an inviting, informative website at *www.rughookingonline.com* and by publishing a number of books on this fiber art. Along with how-to pattern books and a Sourcebook listing of teachers, guilds, and schools, *Rug Hooking* has produced the competition-based book series *A Celebration of Hand-Hooked Rugs*, now in its 15th year.

   The hand-hooked rugs you'll see in *The Secrets of Planning and Designing Hand-Hooked Rugs* represent just a fragment of the incredible art that is being produced today by women and men of all ages. For more information on rug hooking and *Rug Hooking* magazine, call or write us at the address on page 2.

Some strips of wool. A simple tool. A bit of burlap. How ingenious were the women and men of ages past to see how such humble household items could make such beautiful rugs?

Although some form of traditional rug hooking has existed for centuries, this fiber craft became a fiber art only in the last 150 years. The fundamental steps have remained the same: A pattern is drawn onto a foundation, such as burlap or linen. A zigzag line of stitches is sewn along the foundation's edges to keep them from fraying as the rug is worked. The foundation is then stretched onto a frame, and fabric strips or yarn, which may have been dyed by hand, are pulled through it with an implement that resembles a crochet hook inserted into a wooden handle. The compacted loops of wool remain in place without knots or stitching. The completed rug may have its edges whipstitched with cording and yarn as a finishing touch to add durability.

Despite the simplicity of the basic method, highly intricate designs can be created with it. Using a multitude of dyeing techniques to produce unusual effects, or various hooking methods to create realistic shading, or different widths of wool to achieve a primitive or formal style, today's rug hookers have gone beyond making strictly utilitarian floor coverings to also make wallhangings, vests, lampshades, purses, pictorials, portraits, and more. Some have incorporated other kinds of needlework into their hooked rugs to fashion unique and fascinating fiber art that's been shown in museums, exhibits, and galleries throughout the world.

For a good look at what contemporary rug hookers are doing with yesteryear's craft—or to learn how to hook your own rug—pick up a copy of *Rug Hooking* magazine, or visit our web site at *www.rughookingonline.com*. Within the world of rug hooking—and *Rug Hooking* magazine—you'll find there's a style to suit every taste and a growing community of giving, gracious fiber artists who will welcome you to their gatherings.—*Ginny Stimmel*